MW00353595

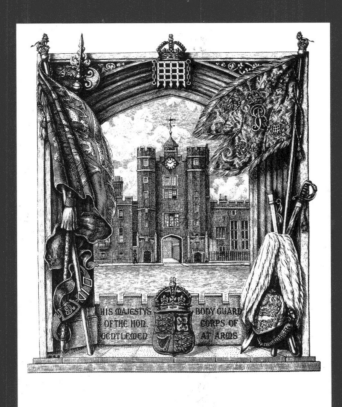

THIS MAJESTY'S BODY GUARD
OF THE HON CORPS OF
GENTLEMEN AT ARMS

THE NEAREST GUARD

500 years of protecting
the Sovereign

Richard and Jan

Another exceptional visit ... a
wonderful festival of Rugby !!

21 March 2010

THE NEAREST GUARD

500 years of protecting the Sovereign

David Edelsten

David Edelsten (signature)

Bene Factum Publishing Ltd

The Nearest Guard – 500 years of protecting
the Sovereign
First published in 2009 by
Bene Factum Publishing Ltd
PO Box 58122
London
SW8 5WZ

Email: inquiries@bene-factum.co.uk
www.bene-factum.co.uk

ISBN: 978-1-903071-26-7
Text © David Edelsten

The rights of David Edelsten to be identified as
the Author of this Work have been asserted by
him in accordance with the Copyright, Designs
and Patents Act, 1988.

All rights reserved. This book is sold under the
condition that no part of it may be reproduced,
copied, stored in a retrieval system or transmitted
in any form or by any means, electronic,
mechanical, photocopying, recording or
otherwise without prior permission in writing of
the publisher.

A CIP catalogue record of this is available from the
British Library

Design and Typesetting by Anikst Design, London
Printed and bound by Latitude Press, Slovenia

Front Cover photograph: Press Association
Back Cover Photograph: Misha Anikst

Contents

BUCKINGHAM PALACE

This new History of the Gentlemen at Arms has been written to commemorate the 500th anniversary of the establishment by King Henry VIII of what he envisaged should be 'a new and sumptuous Royal Guard'.

The evils against which the Sovereign required protection in 1509 have, I expect, changed a little over the years but the loyalty of the Body Guard remains undimmed. As individuals, the Gentlemen have given long and distinguished military service to the nation. As members of the 'Nearest Guard', their service to the Crown continues in a distinctive way and reinforces the very best values of those who came before.

It is more than twenty years since I presented the Honourable Corps with their current Standard. In June 2009, I was pleased to attach to it a unique commemorative Riband to mark half a millennium of faithful service. I asked that it should be guarded and honoured well in the tradition of our forebears, and that it be paraded with pride on the great occasions of State.

This lively story of the Nearest Guard will serve as a reminder of the rich panoply of British history in which the Gentlemen played so central a part. It should also be an inspiration for generations to come.

So I commend this book to readers of every walk of life, and wish the Gentlemen at Arms a long and prosperous future at the end of their splendid first five hundred years of service to the Crown.

Elizabeth R

The Nearest Guard could not have published without the support of many people. Considerable thanks must go the following:

First, the author David Edelsten has been extremely generous with his time in researching and writing this book as well as with his ongoing enthusiasm for the whole project.

Misha Anikst, of Anikst Design, has also been more than generous with his time and professional services taking many of the photographs and subsequently designing the book.

From the Honourable Corps – many have assisted but in particular Lieutenant Colonel the Hon Guy Norrie (Lieutenant), Colonel Sir William Mahon, Bt (Standard Bearer), Colonel Michael Robertson MC, Major John Rodwell and the Axe Keeper Mr Pat Verdon deserve to be mentioned by name.

Mark Henderson, Chairman of Gieves & Hawkes, must be warmly thanked for sponsorship, and Garry Carr of Gieves & Hawkes has been very patient in preparing the uniforms for photography.

David Baldwin, RVM, Serjeant of the Vestry of Her Majesty's Chapels Royal, unearthed some interesting historical nuggets and has taken a most helpful interest throughout.

A book such as this is also made by the illustrations and photographs and these are reproduced by kind permission of the following: Her Majesty Queen Elizabeth II – The Royal Collection, The Bridgeman Art Library, Ministry of Defence, Headquarters London District (Sgt Ian Houlding), Ministry of Defence Art Collection, National Museums Liverpool, Press Association, Steve Solomons, Mr J K Wingfield Digby of Sherborne Castle, Victoria & Albert Museum London.

Specific picture credits p221.

Preface

The Honourable Corps of Gentlemen at Arms, the Sovereign's Body Guard, was established by King Henry VIII as one of the earliest acts of his reign. Its fighting role, witnessed by the two battle honours from that age emblazoned on its Standard, to an extent lapsed with the arrival on the Throne of a nine-year-old consumptive boy, followed by three Queens, and a King who could not bear the sight of a drawn sword. 'Security' gradually, but as we shall see, not entirely, gave place to ceremony as the Body Guard's primary function. However it remains to this day a military body, uniformed and under arms.

Its characteristic weapon, its trademark you might say, is a fearsome battle-axe or halberd, more properly a poleaxe, that, in its present form, dates from the early 18th century, its uniform that of a Heavy Dragoon Guards officer of about 1840. Its home, Head Quarters, Armoury, Orderly Room and Mess are off Engine Court, St James's Palace.

The Body Guard comprises a Captain, Lieutenant, Standard Bearer, Clerk of the Cheque & Adjutant, Harbinger, Axe Keeper and twenty-seven Gentlemen at Arms. All except the Captain, who is a political appointee, are retired Army or Royal Marine officers. They and their predecessors have been at the heart of monarchy throughout twenty-two reigns, proud to be its 'Nearest Guard' for almost a quarter of the entire Christian era.

A Fighting Force

HENRY VIII – ELIZABETH I: 1509 – 1603

It is not easy to look beyond the images of King Henry VIII left us by Hans Holbein, history books and schoolroom memories, to the brilliant youth who ascended the throne at the age of eighteen in 1509. By 1547, he had become "a revolting, swollen mass of putrefying flesh, too heavy for his legs to carry him"[1], yet as little more than a boy he carried on his broad young shoulders the hopes of much of the Christian world.

We can picture him, and get a very good idea of how important *presence*, appearance and martial vigour, were in Renaissance Europe, through word sent home by an ambassador at the time. "His Majesty is the handsomest potentate I have ever set eyes on; above the usual height, with an extremely fine calf to his leg; his complexion fair and bright, with auburn hair combed straight and short in the French fashion, and a round face so very beautiful that it would become a pretty woman. He speaks French, English, Latin, and a little Italian, plays well on the lute and harpsichord, sings from a book at sight, draws the bow with greater strength than any man in England, and jousts marvellously"[2].

"The end of history" was how Thomas More described the young king's coronation, it would "wipe the tear from every eye and put joy in the place of our long distress". If this was to prove to be a less than accurate prophecy in his own case it no doubt reflected feeling at the time: there never was before, nor perhaps ever has been – although those of us with memories that go back to June 2nd 1953 might demur – a more brilliant or indeed popular accession. It was into this world of splendour and high expectation that the Body Guard[3], as we know it today, was born.

King Henry VIII, (1491-1547) who founded the Body Guard in 1509. This painting in the Royal Collection, after Hans Holbein the Younger, was probably acquired by Charles I.

There had been Royal guards before of course, every previous monarch without exception had needed 'close protection'; but "one of the earliest acts of his reign was to establish a new Royal guard, recruited from a higher class of his subjects, and exceeding in magnificence and expense any contemplated by his predecessors"[4].

It was not only in the way that he dressed his hair that the young king took his model from across the Channel, from his enemy at that time in fact, he modelled his 'Speres', or Men at Arms, as they were at first called, on the body guard that had been established some thirty years before by King Louis XI. Soon they even took the identical name of *Pensionnaires*, or Pensioners, denoting that they were members of the King's Household, having a table at Court.

The detail of their enrolment is of interest, if the language is puzzling. "This year the King ordered fiftie Gentlemenne to be Speeres, every of them to have an archer, a demi-launce, and a custrell, and every speere to have three great horses, to be attendaunt on his personne". A demi-launce was a foot-soldier armed with a short spear, a custrell, a sword-carrying attendant, and a great horse, a stallion, albeit in those days no taller at the wither than a modern polo pony. Being a member of the Body Guard, then as now, was evidently no sinecure, it meant expense, as well as honour and duty.

The Earl of Essex (see page 22), the young king's cousin, was the first Captain, and Sir John Pechie his Lieutenant. It was necessarily a force of cavalry, since the King would ride to war, but it was required also to operate on foot. Within four short years it was to be tested in battle[5].

The iconography of King Henry's reign is extraordinarily abundant. Sadly, the pictures most specific to the Body Guard story, a series of enormous paintings commissioned by Sir Anthony Browne (see page 23), the Guard's second Captain, and the only commoner ever to hold that office, were lost when his seat, Cowdray House, was gutted by fire in 1793 (see page 23). Its shell still stands, a scenic backdrop to today's mounted encounters on Cowdray's Lawns.

The Battle of the
Spurs. Flemish School,
painted about 1513 for
Henry VIII.

The Bataile of
Spurs anno
15

A Fighting Force

However, engravings of the series exist that are perhaps more accessible than the originals could ever have been. Studying them, one gets completely lost in the detail, the lively incidents depicted, and their humour. They are a priceless survivor, an endless source of interest.

The Battle of Guinegatte on 16th August 1513, known to most of us as the Battle of the Spurs, unkindly so called because of the alacrity with which the French cavalry quit the field, was the new Guard's first blooding. History does not tell us exactly who did what on that day, but a surviving picture of the battle in Hampton Court Palace shows the Body Guard in action.

We may be sure that his new creation pleased the young King, for it was to be on hand at every great occasion through his reign. Most notably perhaps, this was at the Field of the Cloth of Gold in 1520 (see pages 26-27) where they played a full and glittering part, competing with and besting their prototype, the *Noble Garde du Corps* and, when King Henry VIII last took to the field, at the Siege of Boulogne in 1544.

Strength and display were essentials of survival in the savage, predatory *realpolitik* of the 16th century. However we may judge Henry the man, he understood that he must be master of his world or go under: he was truly a king for his time. His Band of Gentlemen Pensioners, his Body Guard, were both lion's claw and peacock feather: his reign saw their spring and, as a fighting force, their heyday.

———

There cannot be many examples of a more abrupt descent in royal succession than that from the monster of tyranny that Henry had become by his death in 1547, to his infant son. But, just as Holbein's portrait gave few hints of what the father had been, his portrait of the nine-year-old, almost baby-faced, King Edward VI belies a character that had its share of, and was to need, both steel and watchfulness (see page 9).

The son of Jane Seymour, "he was an invalid child, intellectually precocious, earnest and severe, with more conscience than his father but scarcely more

The Execution of Lady Jane Grey painted in 1833 by , Hippolyte (Paul) Delaroche (1797-1856).

King Edward VI (1537-53), son of Henry VIII. It has been suggested that the painter of this work was William Scrots who was employed by Henry VIII from 1545.

Queen Mary I (1516-1558) and Princess Elizabeth (1533-1603) entering London in 1553. This picture depicts Queen Mary wearing a remarkable pearl that was possibly given to her by Philip II of Spain at their wedding in Winchester (where it is recorded that the dancing of the then Lieutenant, Lord Bray, was so admirable that it put "the Spaniards out of countenance"). However, there may have been some artistic license in this fresco from the Houses of Parliament as Queen Mary actually married Philip in 1554 - a year later than the incident shown.

softness of heart"[6], or, to quote a less charitable view, "he was self righteous and downright cruel... (with)... all the makings of a theological prig"[7].

If historians disagree as to his character, we know what the young King thought of his Body Guard, we have his own word for it in his diary, that he "held them in special favour and relied upon them"[8].

Indeed, they were soon in the field again, this time on surrogate duty, against the Scots, at the Battle of Pinkie, on September 10th in the very year of his accession. They were guarding not the Sovereign but the Protector, the Duke of Somerset, which may be why the battle, a decisive victory, does not appear as an honour[9] on their Standard; more probably it is because of the internecine nature of the battle, which, incidentally, also had a naval element.

An episode involving the Body Guard that was perhaps more characteristic of a brief reign fraught with tension, treason and peril, was when, in 1550, that same Protector turned traitor. All available loyal troops were mustered in Hyde Park to forestall an expected *coup*, which however failed to materialize. The young King described his Body Guard on that occasion as "well armed men, their horses all fair and great, the worst worth at least twenty pounds. Thus they careered twice round St James' Field, and so departed"[10].

The Body Guard attended at the young King's coronation, shared his amusements, accompanied him in his progresses, and kept watch over his body when it lay in Westminster Abbey. Since the lying-in-state lasted full five weeks, from the day of the king's death, through Queen Jane's brief reign and Queen Mary's troubled accession, and no candles were allowed as they were considered to be papist, the vigils must have been onerous for the twelve Gentlemen involved, and their reliefs[11].

Edward VI's was thus the reign (1547-1553) that saw the Body Guard for the first time run the full gamut of its court and campaign duties: the father's creation being emphatically seconded by the son.

Elizabeth I (1533–1603).
British School, painted
1580–1585. First recorded
in the Royal Collection in the
reign of William IV.

Through the six nightmare years of what one historian has called 'The Maryan Tragedies' the Body Guard was much in royal favour, and did some good work.

It was of course a time when religious intolerance was at its zenith. All classes of citizens found themselves ordered in the name of King Edward VI to march in one spiritual direction, only to be given the about-face under Queen Mary, any dissent carrying the threat of "the gibbet or the stake"[12].

It is pleasant to record however that Queen Mary, so strict in that regard elsewhere, made few demands of religious conformity on her Pensioners, though the majority were of the Protestant faith. Edward Underhill (see page 30) was a striking example of this benign paradox, an outspoken Calvinist, he never knew her displeasure or discouragement. His vivid account of the Body Guard's role in Sir Thomas Wyatt's dangerous insurrection of 1554 survives; let it suffice to carry the story through this brief unhappy reign.

"The Queen and her people at Court were in great consternation when Wyatt was come to Southwark with his army, intending to enter London that way. The Gentlemen Pensioners were commanded to watch in armour that night, for the protection of the Queen's person; and they came up to the Presence Chamber, with their poleaxes (see page 28) in their hands; whereat the ladies were very fearful, some lamenting and wringing their hands, and said 'Alas! There is some great mischief towards us! We shall all be destroyed this night! What a sight this is to see the Queen's Chamber full of armed men; the like was never heard of'"[13].

Of this occasion it was said that "the pensioners did notably guard the Queen's person when others for fear fled away"[14]. Wyatt's rebellion was of course intended to forestall the 'Spanish Marriage', of the Queen of England to the future King Philip II of Spain. When this in fact took place, at Winchester in July of the same year, Edward Underhill tells us that Lord Bray, the Lieutenant, "put the Spaniards out of countenance with his dancing".

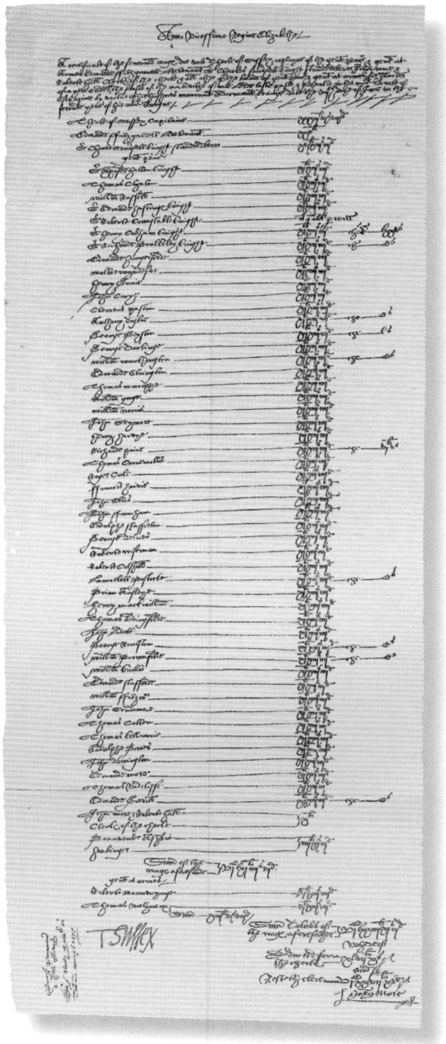

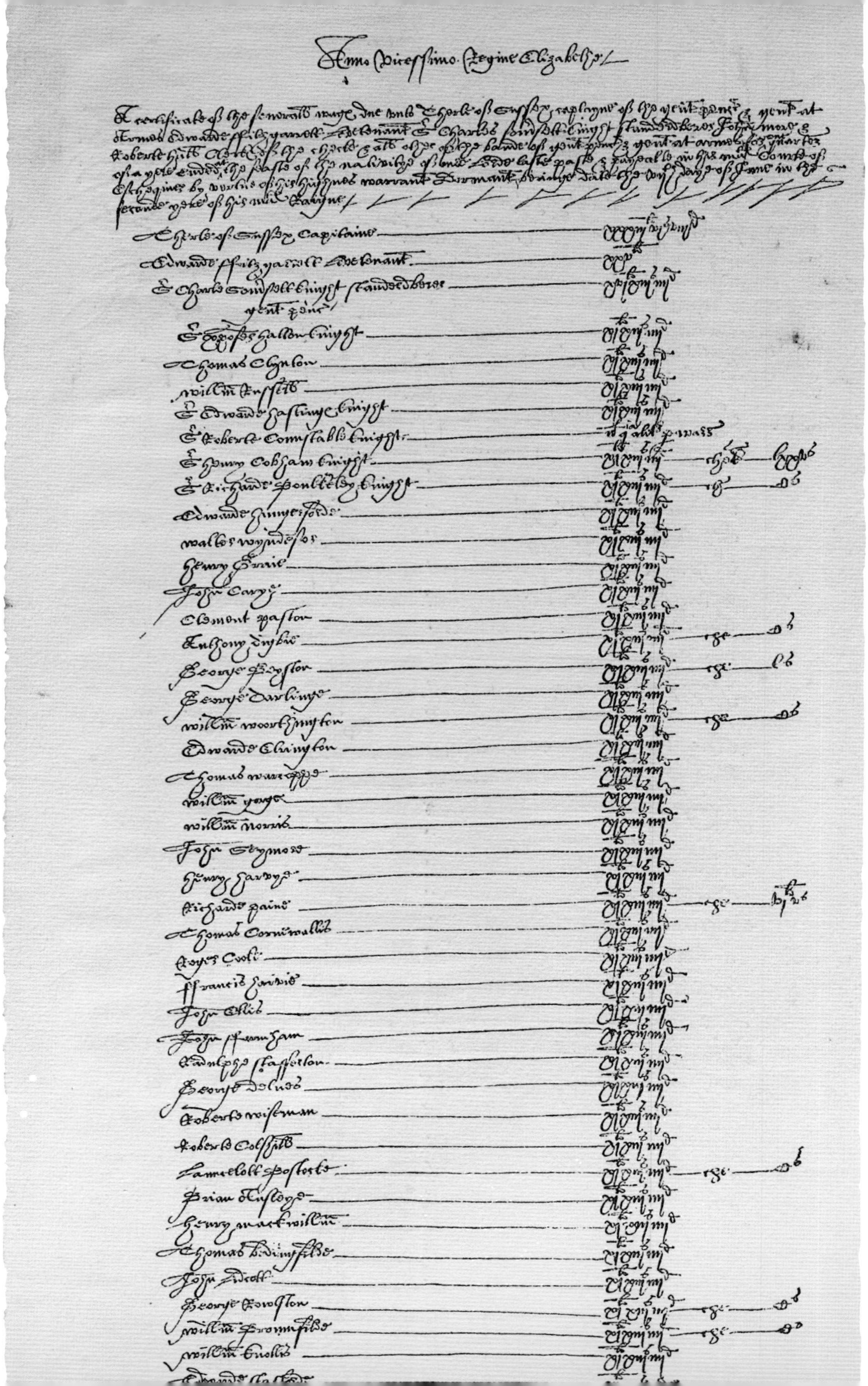

left

Lt Col John Glas Sandeman (for service details see page 80) was a historian and collector. He had in his possession the original Payroll of the Gentlemen Pensioners of 1577-8. The document was annotated by Sandeman, who was evidently something of a comedian, '*A paye rolle of ye Gentlemen Pensioners 1577/8, presented by Lt Col John Glas Sandeman taken from ye original in his own possession, with a faire copie of ye same easie to be understanded made by Lt Col Herbert Mildmay, 1906.*' (Lt Col Herbert Mildmay. Late Rifle Brigade, a Crimean and North West Frontier veteran). Another, original Payroll, dated 1618, on vellum, hangs in the Orderly Room. It has not been transcribed, and is not '*easie to be understanded*'. It, too, was presented by Lt Col Sandeman.

The first Elizabethan age, the sunburst that gave birth to Drake's circumnavigation and to Shakespeare's plays, for the first time, and irremovably, placing the finger of world history on this small island, was also a halcyon time for the Body Guard.

"Elizabeth I was twenty-six when she came to the throne, a tall young woman of commanding presence with auburn hair and piercing grey-black eyes. She was to reign longer than any other Tudor, forty-five years in all"....

"This was an age whose whole stress was on order, rank and degree and a deep fear of anything or anyone who might upset it. Obedience to higher powers was its watchword"[15] – it was also the age of the courtier.

It is scarcely an exaggeration to say that the young Queen delighted in her Body Guard, and why would she not? Until her unhappy childless half-sister died she had lived, since the cradle, in the shadow of the block, surrounded by dangers and distress, her mother executed, herself declared illegitimate. In effect a life-long prisoner, she was suddenly, on that November day in 1558, when the news arrived at Hatfield from St James's Palace, free, secure, a cynosure, devotedly attended.

The records do not tell us exactly where the Pensioners were quartered in the early years of their history. We may take it, however, that their 'table' would have been close at hand, if not actually under the same roof as that of their Sovereign. Thus Greenwich Palace, Henry VIII's birthplace, where he spent his boyhood, and a favourite among the fifty-five palaces of that lavish monarch, must have been their first home.

What we can know for certain is that by 1588, when Queen Elizabeth had her war-room in the Royal Closet of the Chapel Royal, receiving news of the Armada's progress along the English Channel from the signal station on the Gatehouse roof, which was the last receiving post of the hilltop Lambarde beacon chain from the South Coast to London, her Nearest Guard would have been in or close to their present quarters in St James's Palace.

A Fighting Force

In the year 1580 Queen Elizabeth honoured Henry Carey, Lord Hunsdon, K.G. her first cousin and Captain of the Honourable Band of Gentlemen Pensioners (Gentlemen at Arms) with a visit to Hunsdon House in Hertfordshire. The picture shows Lord Hunsdon carrying the Sword of State before the Queen, and Gentlemen Pensioners with their Axes lining the way. The original painting was made at the time by command of Lord Hunsdon.

Let one picture and the life of one 'personage' tell the story of this reign. The picture (see page 16), a breathtaking image, worth any length of journey to set eyes on, hangs in the Red Drawing-room at Sherborne Castle. It is an imaginary, idealized, possibly intentionally iconic view of an improbably young Elizabeth being carried in procession by her courtiers. Her Pensioners, identified by their axes, are much in evidence, as they were, daily almost, throughout her time upon the Throne.

The 'personage', we borrow the word from one of the histories in order to avoid 'celebrity' although we are evidently addressing a similar phenomenon, was Sir Christopher Hatton (see page 31). As a young man studying law at the Inner Temple he caught the Queen's eye, "danced his way into her heart" according to Sir Edmond Chambers[16], became her favourite. He was enriched by her, appointed to the Body Guard (but was not its Captain as some authorities state), and eventually, was, somewhat controversially, elevated to the Woolsack as her Lord Chancellor.

We cannot possibly know, and it would be fruitless, not to say foolish, to speculate as to the nature of this relationship. Certainly the tone and intimate wording of their letters to each other is startling; but what do we know today of the conventions of 'courtly love'?

Look at that Sherborne Castle picture again, the extravagant dress and poses tell us surely that, on the surface at least of Elizabethan court life, they were acting out a fairy, or should we say a *faerie*, story? Whatever the hard reality of those days, we need have no doubt that they were great days for the Body Guard. If the father's reign saw its heyday as a fighting force, *this* daughter's saw its courtly apogee.

Nonetheless the Band, as it was at that time often called, was, as it still is, essentially a band of warriors, men of established military worth and character. William Hervey (see page 32) stands out, his life touching those of the avatars of the age: he is said to have personally strangled an Armada admiral in hand-to-hand combat, knew William Shakespeare, and was possibly the dedicatee of his sonnets.

right

A View of Greenwich, 1632. Painted by Adriaen van Stalbemt (1580-1662) with Jan van Belcamp (died c.1652) for King Charles I. Queen Elizabeth I reviewed the Band of Gentlemen Pensioners at Greenwich, commenting favourably on their mounts, especially the mules and gennets. Greenwich Palace was the favorite haunt of the Tudor monarchs; Henry VIII, Mary and Elizabeth I were all born here. The broad outlines of the Tudor palace can be made out: to the left the remains of the Friary (little more than a rectangular space), built c.1481; the main block running along the river front; to the right Henry VIII's tilt-yard, with the two towers linked by a gallery for spectators. In the bend of the Thames and at the mouth of the Lea, is Blackwall, the site of a shipyard and mooring for large ocean-going vessels (a few visible here), especially those owned by the East India Company. It was from here that Captain John Smith sailed for America in 1606; the East India Dock occupied this site from 1806 until 1967. The field over the river is the site of the O2 Millennium Dome.

Hampton Court Palace about
1640. British School.
Acquired by King George V.
Much of the Body Guard's
Tudor era duty took place at
Hampton Court.

The Earl of Essex

The Body Guard's first Captain: 1509-1526.

We know little enough of the detail of the life of the first Captain of King Henry VIII's new 'Band of Speres', we don't even know when he was born. Such detail as we have however, is strongly suggestive of his character and of the times he lived in.

Henry Bourchier, 2nd Earl of Essex, was one generation removed from the young King he served, being first cousin to his mother. He was a member of Henry VII's Privy Council, and was present at the Siege of Boulogne in 1492, whilst the future king, who was to besiege Boulogne in his turn, was yet in his cradle. We may take it that the Earl was at the very least approaching forty years of age, an 'uncle' figure, when Henry appointed him Captain of his "new and sumptuous Troop of Gentlemen".

Despite the difference in ages, the young King and the Captain of his Band seem to have been kindred spirits. Essex "took a prominent part in the revels in which Henry delighted. Constant reference may be found in the State Papers to the Earl's share in these entertainments. For instance, in 1510, he and others, the King amongst the number, dressed themselves as Robin Hood's men in a revel given for the queen's delectation".

He commanded the Band at the Battle of the Spurs, in 1513, and at the Field of the Cloth of Gold, in 1520, and, between-whiles, was frequently employed in state business and ceremony, such as the formal reception of important visitors, much as the Body Guard is today. These duties evidently put him to some expense: we learn that at one time his tailor had difficulty getting his bills settled.

The manner of his death is perhaps the most telling detail to survive. He broke his neck, being thrown from a young horse, in 1539, when, by any calculation, he must have been approaching his seventies. Having no male issue, his earldom died with him: it was revived when his daughter Anne's husband, William Parr, the King's brother-in-law and the Band's third Captain, was created Earl of Essex.

Source: The Oxford Dictionary of National Biography.

Sir Anthony Browne & Cowdray House
"A most gallant soldier"

Sir Anthony Browne KG

Sir Anthony Browne was Captain from 1526 to 1541. Appointed 'Esquire of the Body' by King Henry VIII in 1524, he became "more and more the friend to his sovereign". When the King was on his deathbed, Browne, "with good courage and conscience" undertook to tell him of his approaching end. He was appointed Guardian to Prince Edward and Princess Elizabeth, carried the news of the young King's accession to him at Hertford, and, as Master of the Horse, rode beside him on his public entry into London.

He himself died in the following year, leaving, in Cowdray House, a splendid series of massive oil paintings of the principal military events of the reign, sadly now only surviving as engravings. He had ten children by his first wife, who lies in effigy beside him on his tomb at Battle. A widower, aged sixty, he married 'fair Geraldine', the fifteen-year-old daughter of the Earl of Southampton, fathering two sons who died in infancy.

Granted Battle Abbey by the King in 1538, he took up residence in the Abbot's lodging, razing to the ground its church, cloisters and chapter-house. It is said that a dispossessed monk cursed his family '*by fire and water*' for this deed.

Four years after coming into the ownership of Battle, Sir Anthony inherited the Cowdray estate from his half-brother, Sir William Fitzwilliam. On his death in 1548 it passed to his son, later to be ennobled as the First Viscount Montague, on the occasion of Queen Mary's 'Spanish Marriage'.

In 1793, in preparation for the 8th Viscount's marriage, whilst he was travelling abroad, extensive refurbishment of Cowdray House was undertaken. Workmen left a charcoal brazier unattended, a fire took hold, fuelled by oil paintings temporarily stored nearby, the building was reduced to the empty shell that it remains today.

The young viscount never returned from his travels, he was drowned in a boating accident on the Rhine. There being no male heir, his sister inherited: her two sons drowned at sea, at Bognor, in Waterloo year.

Sources: DNB and 'Cowdray Ruins' by Liz Higgins.

The Field of the Cloth of Gold
PR triumph – Diplomatic disaster?

previous page
Embarkation of Henry VIII.
British School, painted
between 1520 and 1540, for
Henry VIII.

below
The Field of Cloth of Gold,
1520. British School,
presumably painted for
Henry VIII.

below right
Francis I, King of Frannce,
1494–1547. Henry VIII's
conversationalist/rival at the
Field of Cloth of Gold. After
Joos van Cleve, first recorded
in the Royal Collection in the
time of Charles I. It was with
Francis I that Henry engaged
in wrestling, and to his fury,
lost. Such was diplomacy.

The climax of the early period of King Henry VIII's reign was reached at the Field of the Cloth of Gold in June 1520, when the young King crossed the Channel to meet his rival, Francis I, for the first time. Henry's main worry, we are told, was about his appearance; he could not determine how he would look best, with his usual beard or without it. At first he yielded to his Queen's persuasion and shaved. But directly he had done so he regretted it and grew the beard again. It regained its full luxuriance in time to create a great impression in France.

At the Field of the Cloth of Gold, near Guisnes, the feasting and jousting, the splendour and panache, the tents and accoutrements, what was to prove the last display of medieval chivalry, dazzled all Europe. However, Henry and Francis failed to hit it off, Henry attempting to outdo Francis both by the magnificence of his equipment and the cunning of his diplomacy.

At one unfortunate moment, relying on his great physical strength, Henry suddenly challenged Francis to a wrestling match, but found himself seized in a lightning grip and forced to the ground. He went white with passion, but was restrained by his attendants. Although the ceremonies continued Henry could not forgive such a personal humiliation. Within a month he had concluded an alliance with the Emperor Charles V, thus forfeiting the French tribute. The upshot was renewal of war with France.

Source: Churchill's 'A History of the English Speaking Peoples' Vol II.

The Poleaxe

The precise history of the fearsome axe or war hammer carried by the Gentlemen today is as elusive as its etymology is potentially confusing. The word 'pole' refers of course not to the weapon's six-foot shaft but to its target: *Chambers Dictionary* gives 'poleax' and 'pollaxe' as alternative spellings, and warns the reader not to trip up over the obvious pun. The hammer at the back of the blade, with its four fell spikes, is designed to pierce the helmet and skull, or 'poll', of an adversary, the spearhead having first disabled his oncoming horse.

As to its history, there is direct evidence only of it being in use as early as 1526, but it seems safe to assume, since Henry VIII formed his new Body Guard in precise imitation of the French equivalent, that, from the start, like the *Noble Garde du Corps*, they were armed with the *Becs de Corbyn* or *Becs de Faucon*, even if their mounted battle role meant that its use at that early stage in their history was purely ceremonial.

The delightful myth that the axes used in later reigns were Armada booty can be no more than myth, but, like all myths, it has some foundation in fact. The Royal Armoury in the Tower was the repository of arms captured from the Spanish, and was no doubt at times drawn on by the Gentlemen. However, the axes used by the Body Guard today date from the early eighteenth century, the blue paintwork on the partisan head being no more than facsimile of the Damascus-work of Toledo steel.

Gentlemen are taught axe drill by the Clerk of the Cheque and the Axe Keeper when they first arrive. The most difficult is funeral drill: a special drill parade is held before the Lying in State, at which the drill is refreshed and standardised under the Lieutenant. The spruced-up drill is then watched minutely, and politely criticised by the Foot Guards Warrant Officer who conducts the rehearsals, no doubt reminding those Gentlemen whose service was not with the Brigade of Guards of their time at Sandhurst.

The axes are lodged in the Orderly Room at St James's Palace, where a selection of them forms an imposing display. They have, since 1782, been the responsibility of the Axe Keeper, one of whose chief functions is to carry them to and from the Gentlemen's Duty venues.

Sources: Brackenbury, Kearsley & Crookshank/Martin R Holmes.

Edward Underhill (*c*.1515-1561)
The colourful and contradictory life of a remarkable survivor.

Born about 1515, in manhood Edward Underhill "caused great offence by his attention to concealed papists and his homilies to worldlings and dicers…", and was known as the 'Hot Gospeller'. He distinguished himself at the Siege of Boulogne, caught the King's eye, and was made a Gentleman Pensioner.

He appears almost to have gone out of his way to have made an enemy of the Sovereign on whose Body Guard he was to serve, and of the Catholic interest; yet would seem to have been tolerated, forgiven even. His most egregious provocation must surely have been having Queen Jane, stand (by proxy) godmother to his infant son, when he was christened Guildford, after Jane's equally ill-fated consort. The ceremony took place in the church on Tower Hill, on July 19th 1553, surely one of the most unpropitious days in England's history. It was the very last day of her short reign,

Thrown into Newgate for publishing a ballad lampooning 'papists' in that same year, he was released at the instance of the Earl of Bedford, whose son, Lord Russell, he had rescued from drowning in the Thames. Despite his incorrigible Protestantism, he played a prominent part as a member of Queen Mary's Body Guard, and has left us telling descriptions of the Wyatt rebellion and the 'Spanish Marriage': he died "in office at a good old age under the more congenial rule of her sister".

Let a telling sketch in his own words bespeak the man, the occasion is Queen Mary's marriage, we are in Winchester, on July 25th, 1555…

"We were the chief servitors to carry the meat… the second course at the marriage of a King is given unto the bearers; I mean the meat, but not the dishes, for they were of gold. It was my chance to carry a great pastry of red deer in a great charger, very delicately baked; which, for the weight thereof, divers refused (to carry). The which pastry I sent into London, to my wife and her brother; who cheered therewith many of their friends".

Sources; DNB, Brackenbury, Kearsley & de Lisle.

Sir Christopher Hatton
More than just a courtier and Royal favourite?

Born in Northamptonshire in 1540, Christopher Hatton went to Oxford at the age of 15, and was entered at the Inner Temple five years later, where, performing in a masque, he caught the eye of Queen Elizabeth. He became her favourite, which he remained until his death. A Gentleman Pensioner from 1564 until he became Vice Chamberlain in 1577, he was made Lord Chancellor in 1577, and a Knight of the Garter and Chancellor of Oxford University in 1588. He died, aged 51, in 1591, deeply in debt, and is buried in St Paul's Cathedral.

Today's Hatton Gardens is a reminder of the location of his London home, famously seized for him by his royal patron from the Bishop of Ely, whose demur provoked the rebuke "Proud Prelate, you know what you were before I made you what you are. If you do not immediately comply with my request I will unfrock you, by God".

He was guyed as a mere figure of fun by Sheridan in *The Critic*, and mocked in his tomb by the poet Gray: both seem to have been blinded to his merits by the meteoric brilliance of his rise and the munificent favours loaded on him. There can be no serious doubt as to the quality of his service to the Queen, or the characteristic shrewdness of her employment of him.

A more balanced view acknowledges his gifts as the Queen's political man-of-business, or 'fixer', his humanity in his judicial dealings, and his patronage of the arts. He was an immensely effective parliamentarian, whilst an MP the Queen's mouthpiece in the House of Commons. 'The invaluable Hatton', was how one historian describes him, saying of his speech in the House of Lords after the defeat of the Armada, "for its eloquence, its emotion, and its stirring, confident patriotism… not unworthy of a place in the treasury of England's best".

There is not a shred of evidence that he was the Queen's lover, but she was devoted to him, and, in his last illness, constantly visited him, taking him broths, and feeding him with her own hand. She gave him the nickname 'lids' (eye-lids), which he used in his letters under the symbol of four triangles.

All-in-all, may we not think of Sir Christopher Hatton as a most engaging and gifted man, an ornament to the age he lived in, a true Renaissance man?

Sources; C.R.N.Routh 'Who's Who in History' & Brackenbury.

Sir William Hervey (*c*.1566-1642)

opposite
A sword of the Dragoon Guard pattern carried to this day by the Gentlemen at Arms together with the poleaxe. See page 140.

Few Gentleman Pensioners can have led more colourful or adventurous lives than Sir William, later Admiral Hervey, Baron Kidbrooke. He first signalised himself, to use the DNB's rather quaint locution, at the time of the defeat of the Spanish Armada, in 1588, during the boarding and capture of the galleass San Lorenzo, the flagship of Admiral Hugo de Moncada.

On Monday, August 8th, the San Lorenzo, which carried 50 guns, no fewer than 450 fighting men, and was rowed by 300 galley slaves, grounded on a sandbank off Calais. Along with one other, Hervey swam to the sandbank on a mission to disable the rudder, then, with shipmates, boarded the vessel and personally strangled the Admiral.

In the ensuing imbroglio, which involved the throwing overboard of any surviving Spanish crew, the release of the galley slaves, and the looting of the galleass by the French, Hervey went missing. He was listed as dead, aged 24, on the Gentlemen Pensioners roll 1589/90, only to re-emerge from Spanish captivity, having himself worked for a time as a galley slave. He was knighted for his services under Essex and Raleigh in the capture of Cadiz 1596. Further distinguished and adventurous service, principally in Ireland, again at one time being taken prisoner, saw him made an admiral and raised to the peerage.

Just before the turn of the century he became the third husband of the Dowager Countess of Southampton, and thus the stepfather of William Shakespeare's patron, the young Earl, although only seven years his senior. Solving a riddle that has defeated generations of literary sleuths, recent scholarship identifies William Hervey with the 'Mr WH', to whom Shakespeare's Sonnets were enigmatically dedicated when they appeared in 1609.

Hervey, who saw three reigns, died in 1642 and is buried in Westminster Abbey.

Sources: DNB; HM Chapel Royal; Ivor Cooke's "William Hervey and Shakespeare's Sonnets".

Turmoil leading to more Settled Times

JAMES I – WILLIAM IV: 1603-1837

The gilded helmet, decorated with a wreath of oak leaves and swags. The diamond cut Garter Star is centred by the Royal Arms and surrounded by the Garter and motto. The flowing 17 inch plume of swans feathers (made by joining together a number of smaller feathers) is supported by a 9 inch metal stem rising from the crown of the helmet.

Had any reminder been needed of the realities that underlay the glittering patina of Gloriana's court it was to be promptly furnished in the opening days of the succession. The Queen died, in her seventieth year, on the morning of the 24th of March 1603: within minutes Robert Carey, brother of Lord Hunsdon, the Body Guard's Captain, was in the saddle and secretly on his way to Scotland to secure the favour of King James I.

It was an heroic ride, an epic of the pre-telephonic age. He made the 400 miles to Edinburgh in two days, his efforts no doubt standing the Body Guard in good stead with the new King. But, as historians agree, King James, having small martial bent, had no great liking for his Body Guard; he removed them from the palace and abolished their table. Also, with the arrival of the Stuarts, we enter a century of the Body Guard's history that is full of complaints about non-payment of their salaries[17].

Considering the involvement of the Percy family in the Gunpowder Plot in 1605, which to this day has the Yeomen checking the cellars before leading the Gentlemen into the Royal Gallery of the House of Lords at the State Opening of Parliament, King James's coolness towards his Nearest Guard is hardly surprising. The monarch who gave us the greatest book in our language, yet was known as 'The wisest fool in Christendom'[18], had appointed Northumberland, the 'Wizard Earl' (see page 57), to its captaincy in that very year!

King James VI and I, (1566-1625), painted by Paul van Somer in 1618. Sold in 1651, but recovered for Charles II in 1660.

King Charles I in three positions by Sir Anthony van Dyck, painted in 1635.

We may regard Northumberland's supposed complicity in treachery, for which, guilty or not, he served fifteen years in the Tower, as an aberration, a touch of Hotspur madness in one of his near kinsmen: there is no record in the Body Guard's long history of any similar attaint. The next eighty troubled years, until William III and James's great-grand-daughter shared the throne, were to prove a severe test of loyalty and cool heads, and one which the Band survived with honour.

Charles I took an entirely different view of his Body Guard from that taken by his father, if he was no better in seeing that it was promptly paid. Soon in his reign we see him complaining "by the want of use through a long security, it was doubted if they would be found as fit and skilful as they should be". He ordered that they be drilled in horsemanship and pistol exercises[19]; as we might say today, he got a grip of them.

He was to need his Nearest Guard, and it duly stood faithfully by him in all the battles of the Civil War, notably at Edgehill (see pages 59-61) and Naseby, the last occasions on which the Body Guard performed its original function, protection of its sovereign in the field. During the Commonwealth (1649-1660) it was scattered, dwindling in numbers to a mere twenty-five. But it was never disbanded, and the remnant were among the first to greet his son at the Restoration.

The Merry Monarch's reign (1660-1685) is not the brightest chapter in our story: Charles II was the only sovereign to consider doing away with the Body Guard. Abolition was seriously canvassed in 1677, as a money-saving measure.

Turmoil, Leading to More Settled Times

King Charles II, (1630-1685). It was painted by John Michael Wright probably in 1661, soon after Charles II's Coronation on 23rd April. The King wears St Edward's crown, is dressed in parliamentary robes over the Garter costume and carries the new orb and sceptre. These were made specially by Sir Robert Vyner, the King's goldsmith as the earlier regalia had been destroyed during the Interregnum.

For a time the fate of the Band was actually in the balance, before the idea of abolition was finally abandoned. It was anyway strangely out of kilter with the King's determination to establish regular armed forces. In fact one of the last public acts of Charles II's life was to review the Pensioners on Putney Heath, on October 1st, 1684.

That these were see-saw, tug-o-war times is well illustrated by lives of two succeeding Captains in Charles II's reign, John Lord Bellasyse of Worlaby, and his nephew Thomas Bellasyse, Lord Fauconberg. The one was too strong in his Roman Catholic convictions to submit to the Test Act, thus forfeiting his office: the other was married to a daughter of Oliver Cromwell.

It was that same see-saw that so swiftly bucked Charles II's recklessly popish brother James II from his throne in the bloodless revolution of 1688, obliging him to give place to a Calvinist.

The arrival of William of Orange on the throne of England marked a departure for the Body Guard. He "did not set much store by state ceremonial; the Pensioners were not frequently called upon to attend him on progresses or public occasions, and he was too firmly seated on the throne to require their services in a military capacity[20]".

The dynastic switch and final confessional settlement signalled by the Glorious Revolution must have been an anxious time for the Band. The new monarch, immediately on arrival in this country, replaced their Captain, Lord Huntingdon, a devoted adherent of the last Stuart King, with a Protestant, Lord Lovelace.

Lord Lovelace in his turn purged the Band of all whose religion, politics or Jacobite connections suggested doubtful loyalty. He did this to such effect that no Officer, and only fifteen Gentlemen, survived in the list signed by him in the following year.

From 1688, we may date the Body Guard's modern history, one of purely ceremonial duties. Although the reign saw the start of a quarter of a century of

Dukes   Dutchesses   York Herald   A Marchioness

th the Cross the Golden   The Sword of Mercy the Spiritual
St Edwards Staff   Sword & the Temporal Sword

Captain of   Capt of the   Gentlemen Pensioners
the Guard   Yeomen

Laris   Laris   Laris

tleman Usher K. at Arms Ld Mayor of   Ld High The Sword
Black Rod   London   Constable of State

Gentlemen Pensioners   The Scepter the   the
                         with ij Dove Crown   Orb

previous spread
The King's Majesty detail
from an old print in the
Gentlemen at Arms mess
depicting a Royal procession,
showing the Gentlemen
Pensioners, complete with
axes in the procession. Whilst
there are many such pictures
which depict particular royal
progresses through the years,
this one is thought to
illustrate the layout of such a
procession in the seventeenth
century, but not to be specific
to any one event.

left
King William III (1650-1702,
in Garter robes, by Sir
Godfrey Kneller. Possibly
part of a fragment from the
wall paintings at Windsor,
preserved by Sir Jeffrey
Wyatville during restoration
work at the Castle.

right
Uniform of the Gentlemen
Pensioners in the reign of
King George II. The current
axes date from before this
period, so the one pictured
here is one of today's axes.

almost continuous continental wars, what had been intended from its inception as a nursery for warriors, a point repeatedly made by and to Tudor and the earlier Stuart monarchs (see page 58), began its evolution into what it is today, a source of honourable employment for military men whose active service is behind them.

⎯⎯⎯ ◆ ⎯⎯⎯

The near century-and-a-half that separated the accessions of William III and IV, was not a happy period for the Body Guard. Queen Anne, described by Roy Strong as "a stout, small-minded woman... with an obsession for tittle-tattle and cards"[21], followed the suit led by her late brother-in-law, indifference, as did the first three Georges.

Queen Anne (1665-1714)
painted by Sir Godfrey
Kneller in 1702-4. Purchased
by HM The Queen.

King George I (1660-1727), by
Kneller in 1715.

Sir Roger Monk.
...'at least one of those Hanoverian faux men-at-arms, the wealthy tallow chandler Roger Monk (1755-1832), survives in grateful and honoured memory today. He joined the Band of Gentlemen Pensioners in 1792, and on 31st May 1805 was appointed Exon of the Yeomen of the Guard. He left "the sum of Twenty Pounds per annum to the Honble. Band of Gentlemen Pensioners for ever, towards the expense of a Dinner annually in honour of His Majesty's Birthday". The bequest now produces two cases of claret annually, courtesy of the Tallow Chandlers Company, drunk in his memory at an Autumn dinner, when his portrait, (dressed as senior Exon of the Yeomen of the Guard in the special uniform designed for the Coronation of King George IV in 1820) is passed round from hand to hand by everybody present'.

A problem that was not to be finally solved until 1861, trafficking of places (see page 62), became commonplace, so much so that "when George IV succeeded to the throne, in 1820, the Corps was composed, almost if not quite without exception, of civilians untrained in the use of arms"[22]. For example, of the 29 new enrolments between 1824 and 1831, one only boasted a military rank, a Lieutenant Hemsley of the 40th Foot.

However, at least one of those Hanoverian *faux* men-at-arms, the wealthy Tallow Chandler Roger Monk (1755-1832), survives in grateful and honoured memory today. He left "the sum of Twenty Pounds per annum to the Honble. Band of Gentlemen Pensioners for ever, towards the expense of a Dinner annually in honour of His Majesty's Birthday". The bequest now produces two cases of claret annually, drunk in his memory at an Autumn dinner, when his portrait is passed round from hand to hand by everybody present.

If the early Hanoverian reigns form a queasy interlude in our story, we need not dwell on them. A corrective was at hand, however, a few vignettes may help us picture them.

The Battle of Dettingen in 1743, during the War of the Austrian Succession, as every schoolboy used once upon a time to know, was the last occasion when an English sovereign fought at the head of his army. "King George's horse bolted, but dismounting, and sword in hand, he led the Hanoverian and British infantry into action against the French dragoons"[23].

As at Guinegatte two centuries before, the French cavalry broke and fled, but where was George II's 'Nearest Guard' in this moment of supreme need, the King unhorsed? It was safe at home, its employment in the field long out of question.

Yet, only two years later, the Body Guard was to find itself stood-to for active service. The Young Pretender had crossed the Border, London was in panic, there was a run on the Bank. In the absence of the Captain, on December 5th the

King George II, (1683-1760) British School. This picture, shows the King in about 1740. (First recorded in the Royal Collection in the reign of Queen Victoria).

Lieutenant, Sir William Wynne, issued the following order, presumably to the Clerk of the Cheque, one George Turner....

"Sir, The rebels having advanced to Derby, the King has signified his intention to set up his Standard on Finchley Common; you are therefore commanded to acquaint the Gentlemen of the Band to be in readiness, with their servants, horses and arms, to attend His Majesty there. I am, Sir, your friend and humble servant, William Wynne[24]*."*

Whatever perturbation and alarm this sudden calling in of an ancient debt may have caused after so many years of military desuetude it was to be relatively short-lived: with Culloden, a no doubt uncomfortable four months later, came a countermand.

It is difficult to imagine the pother the order must have caused, impossible to know how far, if at all, the Band got towards rallying on Finchley Common.

No British sovereign can have been in greater need of bodyguards than was George III, nor have shown more admirable *sangfroid* when life and dignity were under threat: we know of at least four such occasions[25].

"The first of these occurred on 2 August 1786, when he was alighting from his coach at the garden front of St James's Palace to attend a levée. A woman named Margaret Nicholson, a domestic servant, approached him, holding a sheet of paper, which he assumed to be a petition. As he took the paper from her she suddenly produced a knife and with it lunged at his chest. The blade of the knife was weak, however, and the blow clumsy. The King was unharmed, and his linen waistcoat scarcely cut; the woman was seized and roughly handled. 'The poor creature is mad' the King protested. 'Do not harm her. She has not hurt me'".

The King was to find himself in far greater danger in 1795 when, on his way to open Parliament, his coach was set upon by a mob. A projectile of some sort penetrated the window glass. "Sit still my Lord", he rebuked one of his companions, who was fidgeting in alarm. "We must not betray fear whatever happens".

left

King George III (1783-1820) by Zoffany. This portrait was painted in 1771 and exhibited at the Royal Academy in the same year. Zoffany's ability to capture a likeness evidently appealed to the King's practical nature and preference for unpretentious art.

opposite above

King George III's Procession to Parliament by John Wootton, painted in 1762.

Whilst it may be questioned why on such an occasion the Gentlemen were not available to prevent attacks upon the King, it was their role, then as now, to be posted in the House of Lords. In this picture, with the procession about to cross Horse Guards Parade, the Yeomen of the Guard can clearly be seen. The picture was purchased for the Royal Collection by King George IV.

Five years later, at a review in Hyde Park, a bullet struck a clerk in the Navy Office who was standing close to the King. When it was suggested that the Princesses should be moved to safety, he said "I will not have one of them stir for the world". That same evening a man fired a pistol at him in the Theatre Royal. Ignoring the advice of the theatre manager, Sheridan, to leave his box, the King peered calmly round the house through his opera glass.

Sheridan, the Gentleman's Magazine of the day tells us, later wrote an extra verse for the National Anthem, which was sung and enthusiastically encored at the Drury Lane Theatre later that year, it ran as follows…

From ev'ry latent foe
From the assassin's blow
God save the King!
O'er him thine arm extend
For Britons' sake defend

Our father, prince and friend
God save the King.

Where was his 'Nearest Guard' on these occasions? As far as we can tell, nowhere near. The term in its original sense had become, for the time being, empty of meaning.

With the arrival of King George IV on the throne, royal neglect, it seems, was suddenly to be replaced by flatulent over-indulgence; "no king since the time of the founder of the band manifested such a passion for splendid apparel and gorgeous pageantry."[22]. Even allowing for the difference two centuries lend to our perspective, it is very difficult, looking at the dress that 'Prinny' put his Body Guard in for his coronation, not to see it as extravagant, effete, effeminate, ridiculous.

It was of a piece, one might say, with the tragicomic pantomime enacted at

right
The Harbinger in Coronation uniform, 19th July 1821. The Harbinger was not an officer, but known as the Gentleman Harbinger. His uniform, as today, included an ivory headed stick.

opposite page
Uniform of a Gentleman Pensioner worn at the Coronation of King George IV, 19th July 1821. This was the dramatic Coronation at which the Queen was refused entry, and a disturbance was caused as she tried to enter Westminster Abbey.

Westminster Abbey's door that day, when his wronged and wretched Queen was refused admission to the ceremony. The records do not tell us what part, if any, the Gentlemen were constrained to play in that tragic farce – Queen Caroline died within weeks – but it is not difficult to imagine their view of it.

George IV's reign also provides us with a telling picture, but of an occasion at which we know from their records that the Body Guard *was* present. It was the funeral of the King's brother, the Army's Commander-in-chief, the Duke of York, in 1827.

The young Home Secretary, Robert Peel, writing to his wife, leaves us an account

King George IV as Prince of Wales by Miltenberg after Gainsborough. His Coronation was the occasion for which the mock tudor uniforms were introduced for the Body Guard. Other participants also found themselves dressed in showy and extravagant new uniforms, especially the pages. The Prince of Wales in this picture of 1782, wears a uniform that was of his own invention, since he was not commissioned into the army by his father until 1793.

of the occasion. "Those attending were kept hanging about for three hours on a January evening before anything happened. The chief mourner was the Duke of Clarence, who, while waiting for his brother's corpse, chatted inconsequently about totals of game shot at this or that weekend. St George's Chapel was in total darkness apart from a few small and grubby wooden chandeliers each holding three wax candles. The mourners, dressed in black, could see little of each other or the service, which was mumbled by the Dean without any attempt at solemnity".

Worst of all according to Peel was the cold. "There was no heating, no carpet, not even a mat or piece of green baize on the stone flags". He advised old Lord Eldon, who had just recovered from an illness, to stand on his own cocked hat as some protection for his frail body from the lethal cold seeping up from the floor.

Emerging from the funeral Canning remarked to Peel that such a performance in a theatre would have been hissed off the stage as contemptible. Casualties from the funeral were said to have totalled two bishops, five footmen and several soldiers [26].

With such Royal insouciance in matters of style and ceremony it is small wonder that the Body Guard in this reign has been described as "at the lowest ebb of its fortunes[27]".

William IV, "the most eccentric and least obnoxious of the sons of George III"[28], who as Duke of Clarence had showed such levity at his brother's funeral, was 65 when he came to the throne, having spent much of his life in the navy – he had entered the service at the age of thirteen in 1779.

"I desire that he may be received without the slightest marks of parade" his anxious father had written, "I trust that the Admiral will order him immediately on board... the young man goes as a sailor, and as such, no marks of distinction are to be shown unto him; they would destroy my whole plan[29]". He was duly entered in the ship's books as an able seaman, the classics tutor who accompanied him as a midshipman.

William IV was to prove a good friend to his Band of Pensioners. He took a

Right
King William IV by Johan Georg Paul Fischer. The Sailor King who instituted the custom of there always being two Royal Marines in the Honourable Corps.

Opposite far right
The Honourable Band of Gentlemen Pensioners by Alexandre-Jean Dubois Drahonet. Commissioned by King William IV. Shows Shako in detail, which features a badge with the Tudor Rose and Portcullis, which was replaced by the Garter Star when the helmet was introduced.

Opposite right
The shako plate bore the Tudor Rose above the Portcullis, as shown in the detail of this painting in the Royal Collection. When the change to helmets was proposed by the Gentlemen, Queen Victoria agreed to this on condition that the Gentlemen themselves wished to adopt the helmet. A vote was held, with three abstentions, and three Gentlemen abroad. The result was almost unanimously in favour of the change, and the decision was taken. An interesting note, in different handwriting in the minute book in the Body Guard archives states 'Officers to continue to wear the cocked hat' ('with Stanloop Cavalry Bullion Tassel and Plume)'. When this was rescinded is unknown. It is also unclear why the ancient Tudor symbols of the Rose and Portcullis were replaced by the Garter Star with the Royal Arms in the centre when the helmet was introduced. Pleasingly, the Portcullis survives on the collar, buttons and tails of the coatee. It seems a pity that the Tudor Rose, symbolising the resolution of conflict between Yorkists and Lancastrians has been lost from the uniforms, thanks presumably to the innovative zeal of Prince Albert. It is interesting also to note that the coatee of the period was double-breasted, as are the present-day coatees of the officers of the Yeomen of the Guard. This suggests that Prince Albert's changes to the Gentlemen's uniform, with the introduction of the Heavy Dragoon Guard's coatee, swept away the old double breasted coatees, which survived unscathed for Yeomen Officers who seem to have avoided his attention, and who still also wear the cocked hat.

minute interest in them and gave them a new title: they were to be known in future as Gentlemen at Arms. They were fortunate also in having at that time, in Thomas Henry, Lord Foley (see page 63), a Captain who was to prove a stout champion, and who evidently hit it off with the elderly king.

We can do no better than to repeat an order that King William sent Lord Foley on December 3rd, 1835, from Brighton…

"The whole of the Officers to be named by His Majesty, who will reserve to himself exclusively the selection of the most proper persons, as vacancies occur, from Lists kept by the Commander in Chief of the Army, who will be responsible to the King for the past conduct and merit of those who may be recommended.

The Lieutenant either to be or to have been a Colonel or Lieutenant Colonel in the British Army or Corps of Royal Marines. The Standard Bearer, the Clerk of the Cheque, and the Harbinger, to be or have been Lieutenant Colonels or Majors in the Army or Marines.

The private Gentlemen to be or to have been Captains or Subalterns in the British Army or Royal Marines, to be selected from the Lists kept by the Commander in Chief and by him laid before the King, who will make his choice both of the Officers and Private Gentlemen of this Corps.

The Officers and Private Gentlemen, if on half pay, are to enjoy the same together with their salaries."

Gentleman Pensioner.

The first mention of the Royal Marines, and indeed the close interest taken by the William IV in his Nearest Guard, which he himself regularly inspected, were no doubt owing to the fact that the country had a 'Sailor King'. At last our story returns from a minor to a major key: the sun breaks out once more: the Body Guard was again valued and under the Royal eye.

Carey's Ride

Through March of 1603, James VI of Scotland was waiting expectantly for news of Queen Elizabeth, then on her deathbed at Richmond Palace. She died at 9am, on the 24th.

All approaches to the palace were guarded, to prevent news reaching James until it should suit the courtiers sitting there in anxious conclave. But Lady Scrope, a Lady in Waiting, who was sister of the Pensioners' Captain, Lord Hunsdon, and of one of their number, Robert Carey, was more than a match for them. Within minutes of the Queen's death she passed the news to her brother, who was concealed below a window.

Carey somehow effected his escape from the closely watched palace, and made such good time on his ride north as to cover 155 miles and reach Doncaster by nightfall. Completing some 400 miles, and taking a severe fall on the way, he reached Edinburgh on the 26th, hailing King James as King of England that afternoon and being rewarded for his heroic effort with a barony: later he was to become the 1st Earl of Monmouth.

Source: Kearsley; Routh

Northumberland & the Gunpowder Plot

A rare case of smoke without a fire?

Henry Percy, born 1564, the ninth earl, was Captain of the Body Guard from 1603 until convicted of Misprision of Treason and committed to the Tower in 1606, where his father had taken his own life a couple of decades earlier.

He had his full share of the Hotspur temperament. As a young man he was imprisoned for causing a disturbance in his mother's house, twice narrowly avoided being involved in duels, was, for a period during their stormy marriage, separated from his touchingly faithful wife, and was once rusticated for spitting in the face of another courtier in the royal presence.

Yet his life, which rewards study, shows him to have been, if colourful in character, wide in his interests and well meaning. But, above all, he could be ill-judged in his actions, was easily led, incapable of keeping a secret. His religion is no mystery, he lobbied hard for tolerance of Catholics but was himself a lifelong member of the established church.

That it was assumed that he had guilty knowledge of the Gunpowder Plot is entirely understandable: things could hardly have looked blacker for him. His cousin Thomas Percy, with whom he had dined on the previous evening, was a principal conspirator: he whom he had appointed a Gentleman Pensioner, covertly dispensing with the Oath of Supremacy against the King's specific order. The only witness who could have cleared his kinsman's name, that same Percy, didn't long survive discovery of the plot – in the earl's words, "none but he can shew me clere as the day, or darke as the night".

Pending trial he was dispatched to the Tower three weeks after the plot was uncovered, and remained there, protesting his innocence, until released in 1621, under the amnesty that marked King James's 55th birthday. He died at Petworth eleven years later on what we have come to call 'Guy Fawkes Day'.

Source; DNB.

Letter From Lord Hunsdon

To King James I

1603

"There are in all Fifty Gentlemen, besides myself, the Lieutenant, Standard Bearer, Clerk of the Cheque, and Gentleman Harbinger, chosen out of the best and ancientest families of England, some of them sons to Earls, Barons, Knights and esquires, men thereunto specially recommended for their worthiness and sufficiency, without any stain or taint of dishonour, or disparagement of blood. Her Majesty and other Princes her predecessors have found great use of their Service, as well in the guard and defence of their royal persons, as also in sundry other important employments, as well civil as military, at home and abroad; insomuch as it hath served them always as a nursery to breed up Deputies in Ireland, Ambassadors into foreign parts, Counsellors of State, Captains of the Guard, Governors of Places, and Commanders in the wars, both by land and sea."

Edgehill
Sunday, October 23rd, 1642.

"O Lord, thou knowest how busy I must be this day,
if I forget thee, do not thou forget me".

If the Battle of Edgehill is chiefly remembered for the recklessness of Prince Rupert's cavalry and the plangent words of his old tutor, Sir Jacob Astley, who commanded the Royalist foot on that field of might-have-beens, we do well to recall the part played by King Charles's Band of Pensioners. They steadied history, saved the day.

When that quintessentially romantic figure, Prince Rupert of the Rhine, son of Bohemia's 'Winter Queen', went haloo-ing off into Warwickshire's Vale of Red Horse with the entire Royalist cavalry, and lost control of them, he, in that moment, also lost his uncle the chance of a decisive victory, effectively lost him the Civil War. But we cannot put the entire blame on the shoulders of a twenty-three-year-old boy. It was not he who ordered, or allowed, the remnant of cavalry left guarding the Royal party to 'join the hunt', leaving one present and two future kings *en prise*.

It is scarcely credible today that King Charles should have taken the Prince of Wales and the Duke of York, aged thirteen and ten respectively, into a field of slaughter that was to see three thousand 'fratricidal' deaths. He may have had no choice, or, perhaps, with their mother in Holland, the centre of his army, under his eye, seemed the safest place for them.

In fact, thanks to the indiscipline of *l'arme blanche*, which was busy sacking the Parliamentary baggage train in Kineton (where, happily, there is an Army ordnance depot today), the King and his two sons found themselves in the thick of the fray, under direct assault, the Royal Standard* captured. "I fear them not", shouted the Prince of Wales, cocking his pistol, before the royal party was hustled off to safer ground.

The contemporary chronicler Clarendon puts a tactful gloss on the incident, telling us that "the King commanded the Prince of Wales and the Duke of York to withdraw to the top of the hill, attended only by the company of Pensioners". One of those Pensioners, Miles Matthews, petitioning for recognition and reward after the Restoration, tells of how he "… with a reserve behind a hayrick, made opportunity for the King and Duke of York to escape… had his horse shot under him, and that the King gave him one of the banners to carry in triumph".

Many Pensioners fell that day, some attending the King, some leading their own levies in the Royalist army. Winston Churchill describes Edgehill as being "marked by abundant ignorance and zeal on both sides", but the Body Guard, as when it stood by Queen Mary in her peril eighty-eight years before, did precisely what it was raised by King Henry VIII to do.

Sources: C.V. Wedgwood 'The King's War', Kearsley & Churchill.

The Eve of Edgehill by Sir Charles Landseer. On Saturday 22nd October 1642, the day before the battle, Charles I held a council of war at Edgecote, about ten miles east of Edgehill. The council was inconclusive because neither side knew where the other was. Indeed, they did not find out until that night when Royalist and Parliamentarian detachments both tried to find sleeping quarters in the same house at Wormleighton.

In this painting, Charles I stands immediately in front of the tree; Prince Rupert is seated; the Earl of Lindsey, the commander-in-chief, has his baton on the map; and Sir Edmond Verney holds the king's standard as he did on the battlefield. On the left are the two young princes, the future Charles II and James II, playing with a dog named Boy (or 'Boye' according to some sources).

Landseer has tried to express the action by pose and gesture. Rupert's self-assurance is shown by having him seated, even in the presence of the king. The bitter rivalry between him and Lindsey is demonstrated by the apparent confrontation between them, which the king is mediating. The King, Prince Rupert the children and the dog all just survived Edgehill, but sadly, Boy was callously shot by the Roundheads after the Battle of Marston Moor.

61

The Trafficking of Places

"O tempora, O mores!"

We should perhaps not be too readily censorious of a practice that looks disreputable to modern eyes but was quite normal and accepted in its day: as Trevelyan tells us, in the 18th century "a 'place' in Church or State was regarded not as a solemn public trust but as a coveted prize". If we may allow ourselves to smile at Lord Foley's horror of *trade* featuring in a would-be Gentleman's CV, we must applaud his part in finally stamping out the *trading* in places that was still commonplace when he became Captain in 1833 (see page 63).

The practice, started under James I, was abolished in Queen Victoria's reign, and finally died out in 1903, when the last Gentleman who had purchased his place, one Colonel F.C.Wemyss, late of the Royal Wiltshire Militia, retired, and when Cox & Kings were formally told that their services were no longer required "in the matter of selling or purchasing Commissions in the Corps, or the stamping of Commissions".

In brief, with the Tudors, a place in the Body Guard became a commodity, one much sought-after, of considerable capital value, to be tenaciously defended against summary expropriation, as in the wholesale expulsion of Jacobites and Catholics from the Body Guard in 1688.

A few figures may give an idea of what was at stake. In Queen Anne's reign, £700 was the value put on the place of Clerk of the Cheque, £500 that of Pensioner. Three reigns later, under George III, when in 1782 Edmund Burke tried, and failed, to have the practice suppressed, the necessary outlay had doubled, £6,000 being the price of the Lieutenancy, £1,000 that of a Gentleman Pensioner, whereas £550 had to be found by a would-be Harbinger or Axe Keeper. By any standards this was big money; we need to multiply those figures some one-hundred-and-twenty times to arrive, approximately, at today's values.

Sources: Kearsley; Trevelyan's 'English Social History'; Bank of England Tables.

Lord Foley

Thomas Henry, Lord Foley, the 4th Baron, succeeded his father as Captain, when the former died in 1833. He was to serve in that office, during the tenure of no fewer than six prime ministers, for 25 of the next 37 years. Perhaps it is not too much to say, that of all the distinguished men, and now women, who have held the office of Captain none did more for the Body Guard, nor more clearly left a mark. He arrived early in King William IV's reign, when there was an Augean stable to be cleared, and, as we shall see, departed having served some many years under Queen Victoria, the job done, lasting reforms consolidated, the Corps established in its royal duties, Mess, dress and privileges, much as they remain today. The Gentlemen have a great deal to thank Lord Foley for.

We know very little directly about his life and character, but some notion of the man and his times may be constructed from a few selected excerpts from the Order Books thus…

March, 1838 – "I have considered it necessary, as well as my duty in consequence of the laxity of discipline I have for some time observed in the Corps, to issue certain Rules and Regulations for the more efficient performance of the several duties".
April 1st 1839 – "No Gentleman shall appear on duty wearing a Moustache or tuft".
1841 – "My attention having been drawn by the Officer on duty, as well as by my own observation,
to the want of attention by the Gentlemen of the Corps to the regular mode of marching and facings, I am anxious to inform the Gentlemen that, unless I observe better attention to this most essential part of the duties of a Military Corps, I shall feel it my duty to re-establish the drill. I must also add that 'talking' after the Gentlemen are once placed on their Stations can on no account whatever be allowed".
January 1st 1848 – The Corps are to parade for the next duty with moustache".
August 1st 1865 – "It being quite contrary to all Military Rules for Officers to wear beards… In future no Gentleman is to appear on duty with a beard".
December 21st 1865 – "The above order is modified. Those in the habit of wearing beards for the benefit of their health are permitted to do so, provided they are not of such a length as to attract general attention".

Source; Kearsley.

Queen Victoria's Reign

1837 – 1901

However distant, and however different from our own times, and however those besotted with modernity may deny it, the Victorian age in great part pegged out the foundations of the way we live today. Although the Body Guard was, just once more, to be warned for armed duty – at the time of the Chartist troubles in 1848 (see page 88) – it soon settled into a routine of exclusively ceremonial duties, or, as Lord Foley put it, "to all that appertains to the splendour of the Court[30]" – and adopted the uniform that is still worn today.

An important series of exchanges between Lord Foley and the Lord Chamberlain in 1851 completed the reforms foreshadowed in the previous reign, finally abolishing the practice of purchase, ending the admission of civilians, and confirming the Body Guard's privileges and principal duties (see page 90).

Before 'Pax Britannica' may be said to have dawned, in Victoria's sunset years, the early decades of her reign had seen unparalleled military activity. Her army fought in thirty campaigns, most of them long forgotten, but including two major wars, during the period of the 'Dual Monarchy'[31], that is to say until the death of Prince Albert in 1861.

What had been designed by Henry VIII as a battle-school for soldiers became under Victoria a working home for war-hardened warriors, many of them decorated heroes. Before we take our story forward with some of *their* stories, let us review the Body Guard's activities through a reign in which it may be said to have found itself again, to have shaken off distempers contracted under the Tudor Monarchy and tolerated, until this latter, happier, time, by the House of Hanover.

L.Waller Wilson

left
Queen Victoria (1819-1901)
by Mrs Koberwein-Terrel,
probably painted for Queen
Mary.

above
State Reception of the
Shahzada by the Queen
Victoria at Windsor Castle,
2nd July 1895. Here the
Queen is presented with the
Ameer of Afghanistan's
letter. (Illustrated London
News 15 July 1895).

An eighteen-year-old girl, Victoria was the youngest Sovereign to ascend the Throne since tragic, fleeting, Jane, whose reign lasted little more than a fortnight (not the 'nine days' of popular legend) in July 1553[32]. Is it too fanciful to suppose that Queen Victoria looked on her Nearest Guard with something of the same eye as had Queen Elizabeth her Band of Pensioners? Both suddenly found themselves exchanging irksome, not to say repugnant, constraint for power and freedom, both needed trusted, older arms to lean on. Certainly she seems to have cherished her Body Guard: certainly it flourished under her benign and interested eye.

Before even the young Queen was crowned, the Gentlemen attended her at a banquet at the Guildhall, given in her honour by the City of London. Then of course they played a full part at her Coronation in 1838, and at her marriage to Prince Albert, in the Chapel Royal, on February 10th, 1840 – both bride and groom but twenty years of age.

It would be tedious to dwell on every note in the grand arpeggio between those early duties, and that great Queen's two Jubilees, in 1887 and 1897, and her funeral in 1901. Suffice it to record that at every Royal family occasion, from the Prince of Wales's Christening in 1842, to the celebration of his Silver Wedding, in 1888; at every landmark in the Nation's life, such as the opening of the Great Exhibition, in 1851 (see picture page 70), and of the Victoria & Albert Museum, in 1899, and on State Visits, such as those by the Shahzada Nasr-ullah-Khan in 1895, and Princess Maud and Prince Charles of Denmark in the following year, the Body Guard was on duty, strengthening internally year by year as the reforms initiated by the Queen's uncle, and endorsed by her Field Marshal Consort and herself steadily took hold.

Let us focus on just two occasions, both, in different ways, unique in their interest for the many, varied and contradictory strands of history and the contemporary scene that they draw together... visits by the King of Prussia, and by the Emperor of France. Both had at one time found refuge in this country, and both had formed friendships with the Queen and Prince Albert.

Kaiser Wilhelm I attended the Christening of the Prince of Wales, which took place at St George's Chapel on January 25th, 1842. The Corps lined the South Aisle, kept guard at the North and South entrances, and provided a four-man Guard of Honour for the Royal visitor. Following the Christening, the Kaiser was invested with the Order of the Garter, the Gentlemen lining the White Drawing Room.

During the three days that the Body Guard was stationed at Windsor we are told, "they were royally lodged and entertained", or, as another authority has it in a pleasing echo of their earliest days "a table was found for them by Her Majesty". (Today, on the occasion of the Garter Service, the Gentlemen make do with, and thoroughly enjoy, a picnic luncheon at their own expense in the private section of Windsor Great Park.)

Napoleon III, nephew of this country's erstwhile greatest enemy, visited in 1855, a valued ally, during the latter stages of the Crimean War. He had visited the

Captain Charles Edward Hopton, late 23rd Foot, the Royal Welch Fusiliers. Wounded at the Battle of the Alma in the Crimea. The earliest photograph of a Gentleman in Uniform. Joined January 1856, resigned 1858.

Great Exhibition in 1851, and the Queen had been to France, twice, including to the Paris Exhibition. The exchange visits were a deliberate attempt by Queen Victoria and Napoleon III to banish for ever the enmity between France and this country. As such, they laid the foundations of the later 'entente cordiale'.

Seven years before, a refugee in this country after two abortive attempts to gain the French Throne, this future French President, by now Emperor, had enrolled as a Special Constable and actually patrolled the streets of London during the Chartist scare.

A delightful picture of him and the Empress Eugenie at the Guildhall survives; he is reading an address. The Body Guard may be seen seated, crowded hugger-mugger together, in a draped balcony, one Gentleman actually perched on the balcony edge, several, it seems, chatting amongst themselves, all apparently 'at

The Opening of the Great Exhibition in the Crystal Palace in Hyde Park by Queen Victoria on 1st May 1851. The Gentlemen at Arms, in their newly introduced Heavy Dragoon Guard style uniforms, were in attendance, and can be seen on the right. After the Exhibition the Crystal Palace was disassembled and taken to Sydenham in 1852. The architect, Paxton oversaw the re-erection of the building and it opened in 1854. It was destroyed by fire in 1936 but the park at Sydenham is still known as Crystal Palace.

The Army List of 1860. When the Gentlemen became once more a military manned organisation they began to feature in the Army Lists. This example shows the roll, with dates of joining, and with a digest of the active service of each gentleman. Those annotated with a small 'p' obtained their position by purchase. Those shown with a heavy P or W served in the Peninsula or Waterloo. It will be recalled that until 1914 the Peninsular War was always referred to as The Great War. These old Army Lists are an invaluable source of interesting reminders of the active service in long-forgotten and arduous campaigns of our illustrious forebears.

123

THE HONOURABLE CORPS OF GENTLEMEN-AT-ARMS,

The Body Guard of the Sovereign on all Public and State occasions.

(ESTABLISHED IN THE YEAR 1509.)

Captain.	*Lieutenant.*
Thomas Henry, Lord Foley.... 28 June 59	Sir William Topham.........p 18 Mar. 53

Standard Bearer.—David James Harmar, p 31 Jan. 48.

Gentlemen-at-Arms.

George Winchester ....p 30 Jan. 38	Charles Richard John Sawyer .. 6 Mar. 56
⊕ John Blakiston¹ (*late Bt.Maj.*) 8 Dec. 43	Harwick Doncaster ....v 6 Mar. 56
⊕ John Henry Cooke² .... 2 Oct. 44	Fred. John Robinson ....p 16 April 56
(*Brevet Lt.-Col. late of 21 F.*)	Lt.-Col. Francis Wheatley ....p 3 June 56
Francis Vanderlure Mills ......v 10 Nov. 48	Stephen Ryder Dampier ......p 19 July 56
Edward Goodwin, *Captain*	(*Capt. Aberdeen Militia*)
Cambridge Militia ....p 22 June 49	John Dutton Hunt ....p 13 June 57
Stapleton Charles Cotton ......p 10 Oct. 49	Sir Henry Orlando Robert Cham-
Charles Tyler ....p 12 Feb. 50	berlain, *Bart.* (*late Lt. 23 F.*) p 24 Oct. 57
Henry Shephard Smyth ......p 24 Aug. 50	Arthur Palliser ....p 22 Apr. 58
Thomas Howard ....p 20 Nov. 50	John Robin Harris ....p 11 June 58
Adolphus Geo. Finch Cotton ..p 21 Jan. 51	Nathaniel George Philips⁶ ....p 9 July 58
Charles James Cox ....p 25 Feb. 51	(*late Capt. 47 F.*)
Markland Barnard ....p 14 May 51	James Lowndes, *Capt. Renfrew*
E. Sutherland (*late Brevet-Maj.*) 26 Feb. 52	*Militia* ....p 4 Nov. 58
Wm. Domvile (*late Capt. 2nd F.*) v 6 Apr. 52	Frederic Stocks Bentley........p 16 Nov. 58
Francis John Helyar........✓..p 26 Apr. 52	Edward Pope Deane ....p 18 Feb. 59
Wm. Handcock Middleton ....v 6 May 54	James Hanning ....p 23 Feb. 59
Charles James Lindam,³ *late of*	Sir Charles Henry John Rich, *Bt.* p 4 Mar. 59
Rifle Brigade .... 19 May 54	Fred. Sykes Daubeney⁷ ......p 5 Mar. 59
Robert Grange ....v 3 Aug. 54	(*late Captain 44 F.*)
(*late Capt. Bengal Army*)	John W. Cheney Ewart ......v 26 May 59
Geo. Bridge, (*Capt. h.p.*)...... 1 Nov. 54	Rich. Hen. Stackhouse Vyvyan,
James W. Cookney ....p 5 July 55	*Lt. Cornwall Rangers*...... v 22 July 59
Arthur Hinton Moore ....p 1 Jan. 56	James Peters ....p 8 Aug. 59
Aug. Sam. Bolton⁴ (*late Capt. 31 F.*) 7 Feb. 56	

Adjutant.—William Walter Cargill, p 10 April 56.
Harbinger.—Samuel Wilson, p 24 Feb. 31.
Sub-Officers.—⊕ Lt.-Col. Cooke, 24 June 48.

Scarlet—*Facing* Blue Velvet.   *Agents*—Messrs. Cox and Co.

* 1 Major Blakiston having passed through the Royal Military Academy at Woolwich in 1802, he proceeded to India as a Cadet in the East India Company's Service, and was appointed to the Corps of Engineers on the Madras Establishment, being then on half-pay as a Lieutenant in H.M. Service. In 1803 he served in the campaign against the Mahrattas, and was engaged in the battles of Assaye and Argaum, and at the sieges and assaults of Ahmednuggur and Gawilghur. At the suppression of the mutiny at Vellore in 1805 he directed the guns by which the gate was blown open. In 1810 he acted as Chief Engineer at the capture of the Island of Bourbon. Having been employed in reconnoitring the coast of the Isle of France previous to the arrival of the expedition, he was instrumental in discovering the spot where the descent was made; and, having been appointed to the charge of the Guides, he led the advance of the Army until the surrender of that Island. For his services on the above occasion he was nominated Extra Aide-de-Camp to the Commander-in-Chief, Sir Samuel Auchmuty, on the expedition to Java in 1811; and having been sent in advance with the Chief Engineer to fix on the point of landing, he was engaged in a serious affair on the coast in the boats of H.M. ships *Barracouta* and *Leda*. On the landing of the Army he was engaged in the affairs of Wellevrieden and Samarang, and at the siege and assault of the fortified position of Cornelis. In 1812, having attained the rank of Captain in the corps of Madras Engineers, he returned on furlough to England. Shortly afterwards, having been placed on full pay in H.M. 87th Regt., he was appointed to a Company in the 17th Portuguese Regt., with which he served in the Light Division of the Peninsular Army until the conclusion of the war; having been present at the battles of Vittoria, Nivelle, Nive, Orthes, and Toulouse, and in all the affairs in which the Light Division was engaged. At the siege of San Sebastian he volunteered as an Engineer, and while so engaged was severely wounded. For his services on this occasion he was promoted to a Company in the 27th Regt.; in 1816 was placed on half-pay; and on the 23rd June 1843 he was brought on full pay of the 51st Regt., and retired by the sale of his commissions. He has received the War Medal with six Clasps; also the Indian War Medal and Clasps.

2 Lt.-Col. Cooke served with the 43rd Regt. at Walcheren, in 1809. In June 1811 he joined the Light Division in the Peninsula, and was present at the siege and storming of Ciudad Rodrigo, and of Badajoz (wounded at the assault), actions of Castrejon and San Christoval, battle of Salamanca, actions of San Munoz and San Milan, battle of Vittoria (wounded), actions in the Pyrenees, siege of San Sebastian, the attack on the heights of Vera, battle of the Nivelle, battles of the Nive on the 9th, 10th, 11th, 12th, and 13th Dec., actions at Tarbes and Arcangues, battle of Toulouse, besides various affairs of less importance. On the 8th Jan. 1815, he was present at the attack on the American Lines before New Orleans. He served afterwards with the Army during the Occupation in France. He has received the War Medal with eight Clasps.

3 Captain Lindam served in the 10th Foot in the Sutlej campaign of 1845-46, and was severely wounded (lost a leg) at the battle of Sobraon (Medal). He served also four years as Paymaster in the Rifle Brigade in British Caffraria, including the Kaffir war of 1846-47.

4 Captain Augustus S. Bolton served the campaign on the Sutlej (Medal and three Clasps). He acted as Aide-de-Camp to Sir Harry Smith at Moodkee and Ferozeshah, and was Adjutant of the 31st at Budiwal, Aliwal, and Sobraon (severely wounded).

6 Captain Philips served with the 47th Regt. in the Eastern campaign of 1854, and was severely wounded at the battle of Alma (Medal and Clasp).

7 Captain Daubeney served with the 55th Regt. on the China expedition in 1842 (Medal), and was present at the escalade and capture of Chin Kiang Foo, where he carried the Regimental Colour, which was shot in two places.

The Queen, riding Sunset, distributing the first Victoria Crosses in Hyde Park, 26 June 1857 by George Housman Thomas (1824-68).

ease' and scarcely attentive. One wonders where their martinet Captain was, and what he had to say to them about it afterwards.

Described by one historian as amiable and dreamy, Louis Napoleon cuts an enigmatic but appealingly anglophile figure. Many readers will remember the Sandhurst statue of his son, the Prince Imperial, who joined the British Army and was killed in the Zulu War.

Who today remembers hearing of the Persian War of 1856/57? That it is clean forgotten, like so much of soldiers' far-called toil, is scarcely surprising, you may look in vain for a reference to it in the index of most history books. What though it shares oblivion with almost countless forays into the near- and middle-east profitable only in blood and lessons never learnt, its significance to our story is that it was on this campaign that Capt John Grant Malcolmson won the Victoria Cross[33].

He was the first of thirteen holders of the VC to earn that peerless accolade, and to bring it with him later to honour the ranks of the Gentlemen at Arms.

When, in 1856, Shah Nasr ad-Din invaded Afghanistan intent on installing a pro-Persian ruler in Herat, war was declared, and an expeditionary force under Major-General Sir James Outram dispatched from Bombay.

The business was soon settled, at the Battle of Khoosh-ab, on Febuary 8th, 1857, which was when Capt Malcolmson, then a Lieutenant in the 3rd Bombay Light Cavalry saved the life of his adjutant. The citation reads, "*observing his peril, (he) fought his way to his dismounted comrade through a crowd of enemies... and giving him his stirrup, safely carried him through everything out of the throng*".

Malcolmson went on to serve in the Indian Mutiny, before becoming a Gentleman at Arms in 1870. Born in Inverness-shire in 1835, he died, whilst still a member of the Corps, in 1902.

———

A cruel surprise awaited Queen Victoria as she rode her horse Sunset back to Buckingham Palace from Hyde Park on the morning of June 26th, 1857, having presented VCs to 62 Crimean veterans. Never having ridden on such an occasion before, it had shown some spirit, in her 39th year, only two months after her ninth and last confinement: how much easier and relatively stress-free it would have been to have travelled in a landau. We may suppose also that it had been looked forward to as an especially happy day. Not only might the occasion be thought of as putting a final seal on a tragic war, but it was also the first public appearance of her beloved husband as Prince Consort, this dignity, after a long wrangle, having at last been approved by the Privy Council on the previous day.

The news that greeted her as she dismounted at the Palace, news that had been a month and more in passage, was of the murder of their European officers by three Indian regiments at Meerut on May 10th, and of Delhi being in insurgents' hands.

If it was the start of a three-year nightmare for the Queen, in detail if not in

left
God Save The Queen': Queen
Victoria arriving at St Paul's
Cathedral on the occasion
of the Diamond Jubilee
Thanksgiving Service, 22nd
June 1897, by John Charlton.
The Gentlemen at Arms can be
seen at the bottom of the steps.

overleaf
The Queen's Garden Party, 28
June 1897. (The Diamond
Jubilee). By Laurits Regner
Tuxen. Commissioned by
Queen Victoria.

scale worse even than the Crimean War, it also began a chapter in her reign that one reads with admiration for the personal qualities she brought to the crisis.

For ever goading the reluctant home government to action during the early stages, she was, as constantly, urging humanity and restraint when the campaign entered its retributive latter phase. Invoking first resolution, then magnanimity, it was a fore-echo, may we not think, of another great exemplar in a later war?

The Mutiny was not to end until the Governor General, Canning (son of George IV's prime minister), was able to declare a 'State of Peace' in July of 1859. Two Body Guard VCs date from the campaign, both from the early part of its second year.

If Palmerston's government was slow in its response to the news from the subcontinent, local commanders, deceived by disbelief and reacting to an incalculable situation, the loyalty of their troops uncertain, missed early chances.

Delhi might have swiftly been retaken had the general on the spot acted more decisively. But through to August the situation steadily worsened, with the unspeakable horror of two massacres at Cawnpore and enduring agony in besieged Lucknow. However, the arrival of reinforcements and better generals brought a turn of tide, and the start of long, painful, too often vengeful, mopping-up.

It was during this phase, in Oudh, that Capt Frederick Robertson Aikman won his VC. His own 4th Bengal Native Infantry having been disarmed as unreliable, he found himself, on March 1st, 1858, at the age of thirty, commanding the 3rd Sikh Cavalry. When, "on the advanced picquet, with one hundred of his men, having obtained information, just as the Force marched... of the proximity... of a body of five hundred rebel infantry, two hundred horse and guns.... attacked and utterly routed them... This feat was performed under every disadvantage of broken ground... and the flanking fire of an adjoining fort."

Exactly a month later, on the River Betwa in central India, Lieut James Leith of the 14th Light Dragoons, having distinguished himself in earlier actions, being

once wounded, twice mentioned in dispatches, and given the brevet rank of major, won his VC *"for conspicuous bravery... having charged alone, and rescued Capt Need of the same regiment, when surrounded by a large number of rebel infantry"*.

Leith, a general's son who played cricket for England, joined the Gentlemen at Arms in 1863. Born in Aberdeenshire in 1826, he died shortly before his 43rd birthday, in 1869. Aikman, who had received a severe sabre cut to the face in his action, a wound that eventually compelled him to quit the service, joined the Corps two years after Leith, in 1865. Yet another Scotsman, born in Lanarkshire in 1828, he dropped dead attending a ball in 1888.

The Queen was twenty years into widowhood and five years short of her Golden Jubilee when the fourth and last of the VCs who were to serve with her Body Guard in her lifetime won the award. It was another Henty-type exploit, in another obscure, forgotten war.

Disraeli's purchase of Suez Canal shares in 1875 had, as predicted by his successor Gladstone, who had to handle them, brought turbulent Egypt's problems in its wake. In 1881, a nationalist revolt led by Colonel Arabi Pasha threatened Anglo-French control of the country, there was a massacre of Europeans in Alexandria, the fleet was sent, the place bombarded, a force embarked.

In the following year, on September 13th, Sir Garnet Wolseley decisively defeated Arabi at Tel-el-Kebir. This was where Lieut William Mordaunt Marsh Edwards, of the 2nd Battalion The Highland Light Infantry (that Scottish connection again!) *"in leading a party... to storm a redoubt... in advance of his party, with great gallantry rushed alone into the battery, killed the artillery officer in charge, and was himself knocked down by a gunner with a rammer, and only rescued by the timely arrival of three men of his own regiment"*.

Edwards joined the Corps in 1899. Born at Hardingham Hall, Norfolk in 1855, he died there in 1912.

The Graphic 7 March 1891.
Debutantes awaiting
presentation, while two
Gentlemen, (depicted with
medals on the wrong side!)
look on. The artist was
Arthur Hopkins, RWS
(1848-1930).

Order by Lord Foley
(Captain) March 1866: 'The
Corps of Gentlemen-at-
Arms, being a Guard on Duty
'under arms,' will stand in a
steady and soldier-like
position at their Posts.
Gentlemen should not leave

their Posts for the purpose of
placing the Company as they
assemble at Drawing Rooms,
Levées, and Court
Ceremonies, but merely give
proper directions as to where
the Company are to place
themselves.'

above

Distinguished Victorian Gentlemen at Arms. Standing to the right right behind the table: Col Sir Gustavus Hume. Seated front row right of table, The Captain, the Earl of Yarborough. Left of table: Lt Col John Glas Sandeman, late Royal Dragoons, the Sub-Officer, who can be seen with the ivory stick but no officer's aiguilettes. He served in the Crimea at Balaklava, Inkerman, Tchernaya and the siege and fall of Sebastopol. Standing behind Col Sandeman is the Lieutenant, Col Sir Henry Oldham, Knt, CVO, late Cameron Highlanders. He wears the China

Expeditionary Force medal 1860 (present at the actions of Sinho and Tangku, assault and capture of the North Taku Fort and the surrender of Pekin). He was also at Cossyah and Jynteah Hill Campaign of 1863 in the Arakan, Burma. Major L Tillbrook stands to the left at the rear. This Gentleman, who joined by purchase, retired on half pay in 1900.

right

Gentlemen at Arms in the Throne Room at St James's Palace by Sir Arthur Felix Temple Clay painted in 1892. This painting with the figures over life size was too large to

be accommodated by the Honourable Corps, and it appears that the artist was unable to sell it as he had hoped. Eventually he presented it, after a long correspondence, to the War Office in 1902. For many years it hung outside the office of the Chief of the Imperial General Staff. It now hangs at a military establishment in Wiltshire. (Picture courtesy of the MOD Art Collection).

The Gentlemen pictured are, from left to right:

1. Colonel JCD Morrison late Royal Marines. Involved on 20 November 1845 Anglo-French expedition up the

Parana River, Argentina, including the capture of the batteries of Obligado. China Expedition 1858, blockade of Canton River. Provost Marshal Canton. Campaign in North China 1860 including Tongoo and storming of the North Takoo Fort (mentioned in Despatches).

2. Lt Col Sir Gustavus Hume
3. Charles Alfred Worsley Anderson-Pelham, P.C. 4th Earl of Yarborough, Captain, 1890-1892.
4. Lt Col George Henry Pocklington, late 18th Foot (The Royal Irish Regiment). Appointed July 1877. Served Burmese campaign 1852-3,

and in the Crimea from June 1855, Siege and fall of Sebastopol.

5. Lord Carrington, later Marquis of Lincolnshire, KG, GCMG. He is wearing the undress uniform of the New Zealand Mounted Rifles, of which he was Colonel. This was the only regiment in the Empire which allowed the wearing of decorations in an undress uniform at that date.
6. Lt Col John Glas Sandeman.
7. Colonel H.H.Oldham.

The five days during the final month of the 19th century that came to be known as 'Black Week' must have seemed apocalyptic to a public newly awakened to the idea of Empire and the achievements of an historic reign by two recent Jubilees. The country needed steadying, needed a lead: the eighty-year-old Queen gave it. "Please understand", she said to Prime Minister Balfour, "that there is no depression in *this* house. We are not interested in the possibilities of defeat. They do not exist"[34].

The second Boer War had started, and started as badly for Britain as a war could start. Kruger's forces having invaded Cape Colony and Natal, investing Kimberley, Mafeking and Ladysmith, a corps of three divisions under General Sir Redvers Buller VC had been dispatched to the theatre. Departing from the pre-concerted strategy of an advance on Bloemfontein, and abandoning just about every Principle of War, Buller sent his force off in three divergent directions, thus contriving possibly the most startling setback in our military history to that date, the defeats of Black Week, at Magersfontein, Stormberg Junction and Colenso[35].

It was at the last of these, on the River Tugela in Natal, that Capt Harry Norton Schofield, one of Buller's three ADCs, won a DSO. This was cancelled two years later and, in response to public outcry, and replaced by a VC.

The story of the exploit that so caught the public imagination at the time bears retelling in some detail. At Colenso, Buller, who had accompanied the right hand of his three ill-fated thrusts, the one directed on Ladysmith, allowed two batteries of field artillery and six naval guns to be ordered forward, within a thousand yards of the Boer trenches. They were completely exposed to direct enemy fire, soon ran out of ammunition and had to be abandoned by their crews.

About 800 yards to the rear of the guns was a donga, or sunken track, in which the drivers and teams were taking cover. Riding this lane, Buller expressed a wish that an attempt be made to retrieve at least some of the guns that had been deployed so rashly.

A Victorian Scene: Opening of the Imperial Institute, as foreseen by the Daily Graphic, 10 May 1893. 'Gentlemen at Arms who will be on duty today in the Great Hall and its porch'. The Imperial Institute building in South Kensington, is now part of Imperial College London, famous for its excellence in the fields of science, engineering and medicine. Only the 287-foot (85-metre) high Queen's Tower remains among the more modern buildings today.

The building was designed by Thomas Colcutt and was originally intended as a national memorial of completion of the fiftieth year of Queen Victoria's reign. The foundation stone was laid by Queen Victoria in 1887, and it was opened by Her Majesty in state on May 10th, 1893. After the opening there was a magnificent peal of bells. The belfry contains the Alexandra Peal of bells, the peal consists of 10 bells and is named after Alexandra, Princess of Wales. The bells were a gift to the Prince of Wales from Mrs Elizabeth M Millar of Melbourne, Australia in 1892. Each bell is separately named after members of the Royal family – Queen Victoria, her three sons, her daughter-in-law Alexandra and her five Wales grandchildren. The bells are now rung on Royal Anniversaries, between 13:00 and 14:00: The Queen's Accession: 6 February, The Queen's Birthday: 21 April , The Queen's Coronation: 2 June, The Duke of Edinburgh's Birthday: 10 June , The Princess Royal's Birthday: 15 August, The Prince of Wales's Birthday: 14 November, The Queen's Wedding Day: 20 November.

Gentlemen at Arms marching through Windsor High Street, outside the London and County Bank, with axes reversed and swords trailing (not carried) in the 1901 funeral procession of Queen Victoria en route for Frogmore. Note the street liners standing shoulder to shoulder.

A contemporary account continues "*Congreve, Schofield and Roberts* (the three ADCS), *were the leaders in this forlorn hope, the latter being the only son of Lord Roberts* (later to be sent out to South Africa as C-in-C). *As soon as the teams were hooked into the limbers on the bank of the donga, Capt Schofield gave the order to gallop for the guns, and, as they got nearer, directed them on to the two on the right, as they appeared to be clear of dead horses.... Roberts joined them... was shot* (wounded fatally)... *Congreve fell wounded... Capt Schofield and Cpl Nurse jumped off their horses and hooked in the two guns, with which they returned. Capt Schofield sustained six bullet wounds in the action*".

This redoubtable warrior went on to serve in many of the major actions in the war, including Spion Kop and the Relief of Ladysmith. He retired the service in 1905, joined the Body Guard in 1911, but re-joined the colours to serve through the Great War. Born in Lancashire in 1865, the son of a JP, he died in 1931, his funeral being held at the Chapel Royal, St James's Palace.

Capt Conwyn Mansel-Jones of The West Yorkshire Regiment was another Gentleman at Arms to serve in both the South African and the Great Wars, in his case coming out of retirement, due to ill-health following his wounds, to add a DSO and the Legion of Honour to his Boer War VC; he was no less than six times mentioned in Despatches. His was surely a scarcely believable record of gallantry. Here, from the citation, is how he won his VC...

"*On 27th February 1900, during the assault on Terrace Hill north of the Tugela in Natal, the companies of the West Yorkshire Regiment, on the northern slope of the hill, met with severe shell, Vickers-Maxim and rifle fire, and their advance was for a few minutes checked. Capt Mansel-Jones, however, by his strong initiative, restored confidence, and in spite of his falling very seriously wounded, the men took the whole ridge without further check; this officer's self-sacrificing devotion to duty at a critical moment having averted what might have proved a serious check to the whole assault*".

The Queen, who had proved herself to be so tough under the hammer of events, and on the anvil of a sovereign's, so public, life, wept when she decorated Capt Ernest Beachcroft Beckwith Towse with his VC in the Throne Room of the State Apartments at St James's Palace. . The story of how he won it, and of his later life, may perhaps form an apt ending to this sketch of an heroic reign.

His citation, which, unusually, covers two actions, reads that, whilst serving with the Gordon Highlanders (transferred from the Wiltshire Regiment we hasten to add) ... *"On the 11th December, 1899, at the action of Magersfontein, Capt Towse was brought to the notice of his commanding officer for his gallantry and devotion in assisting the late Colonel Dowman, when mortally wounded, in the retirement, and endeavouring when close up to the front of the firing line, to carry Colonel Dowman on his back; but finding this not possible, Capt Towse supported him until joined by Colour-Sergeant Nelson and LCpl Hodgson.*

On the 30th April, 1900, Capt Towse, with twelve men, took up a position on the top of Mount Thaba, far away from support. A force of about 150 Boers attempted to seize the same plateau, neither party appearing to see the other until they were but one hundred yards apart. Some of the Boers then got within forty yards of Capt Towse and his party and called on him to surrender. He at once caused his men to open fire, and remained firing himself until severely wounded (both eyes shattered), thus succeeding in driving off the Boers. The gallantry of this officer in vigorously attacking the enemy (for he not only fired, but charged forward) saved the situation; notwithstanding the numerical superiority of the Boers".

Despite his blindness, Capt Towse, who joined the Gentlemen at Arms in 1903, returned to the colours during the Great War, and became a well-known figure at the base hospitals in France, where he used his skills as a typist to write letters for the wounded. He was Mentioned in Despatches and awarded an MBE at the war's end.

With peace, he turned his energies to the service of the blind, travelling the length and breadth of the country to help the British and Foreign Blind Association, and to foster public interest in the welfare of blind people, founding a fund, launched by Winston Churchill on Christmas Day 1929, to provide wirelesses for them.

Whilst a Gentleman at Arms, Sir Beachcroft, as he then was, fulfilled all the normal duties, in uniform, being led to his post by the next-for-duty Gentleman. He was present at the 400th Aniversary Parade at Buckingham Palace, and was remembered at the 500th by the playing of an arrangement of the pipe tune named after him.

The Chartist Riots

An early example of 'Rain stopped play'?
1848

If some historians discount the Chartist upheavals as a non-event – Trevelyan does not even mention them – they caused considerable perturbation at the time, and they throw a revealing light on the then condition of the Body Guard.

The so-called 'Riots', though they hardly deserve the name, had their roots a decade earlier, in the second year of Queen Victoria's reign, when a group of working class leaders put together a 'People's Charter', demanding, amongst other things, universal male suffrage and the secret ballot. Churchill describes it as "the last despairing cry of poverty against the Machine Age". Gelded by Victorian prosperity, the movement never really caught on.

Through the 1840s there were meetings, petitions and demonstrations, and indeed riots, in Birmingham, put down by force. It all but fizzled out, only to flame again in 1848, Europe's 'Year of Revolutions', when just about every continental Crown was at least shaken, some fell.

The Government's and the Palace's concern, when a massive meeting on Kennington Common was called for April 10th, was therefore understandable. In the event, more spectators than demonstrators turned out, and a proposed march on Westminster, when forbidden by the police, was tamely cancelled. The Duke of Wellington, still Commander-in-Chief aged 78, commented that the English are "a very quiet people" – "This is especially so when it is raining", added Churchill dryly, writing a century later.

Meanwhile, on April 7th, the Captain, Lord Foley, received what we would call a Warning Order from Lord Spencer, the Lord Chamberlain. The Gentlemen were to "take charge of the interior of St James's Palace, for the protection thereof". Next day, a private letter between the two amplified these instructions, ending "I hope that everything will go off quietly".

On the day itself, Kearsley tells us, all the Officers and Gentlemen "paraded in the State Rooms… where they found that 100 muskets and powder had been delivered… (but)… only three Gentlemen in the Corps had any military experience… Majors John Blakiston (see page 89), John Cooke, and Percy Neville… (all three Peninsular veterans, Major Neville had also served at Waterloo)… These three hurriedly explained to the others how to handle and load their muskets…. Luckily the day passed off quietly and the Corps was dismissed in the evening".

If the Chartists achieved nothing else that day, may we not credit them with prompting Lord Foley to apply whip and spur in his reforming zeal? The Chartists' own, to our eyes, so reasonable demands were all to be met in the following century.

Sources: Churchill; Strong; Kearsley.

Major John Blakiston (*c.1782-1867*)

appointed to a company in the 17th Portuguese Regiment which served in the Light Division in the Peninsular War. He was present at the battles of Vittoria, Nivelle, The Nive, Orthes and Toulouse and was present at all the affairs in which the Light Division was engaged. At the Siege of San Sebastian he volunteered as an engineer officer, and while so engaged was severely wounded. For his services on this occasion he was promoted to a company in the 27th Regiment. In 1816 he was placed on half pay. On 23 June 1843 he was brought onto full pay of the 51st Regiment, and retired by sale of his commissions. He received the War Medal (i.e. the Military General Service Medal) with 6 Clasps, and the Indian War Medal 'and clasps'".

We copy below the Army List biography (see page 71) of this remarkable warrior...

"India 1802, Assaye, Argaum, Ahmednuggar, Gawihghur. Vellore 1805, Capture of Isle of Bourbon. ADC to C-in-C Java Expedition 1811, including opposed amphibious landing. Furlough in England as Capt Madras Engineers, he took a commission in the 87th Regiment and was

The Body Guard's Privileges

Gentlemen at Arms on duty for The Queen's Court 9th June 1866, at Buckingham Palace. Among other information the original caption stated ' They have the right also to wait at the royal dinner on Coronation days.

The following was the list of Privileges agreed by Queen Victoria, following an exchange between Lord Foley and the Lord Chamberlain in 1851:

1. Of attending the Sovereign upon State and Domestic occasions in the Palace and out of the Palace in times of trouble as well as of peace as the immediate Body Guard of the Sovereign.

2. Of being "*The Nearest Guard* and the *Principal Military Corps* of the Household".

3. Of under all circumstances when on duty together with the Yeomen of the Guard taking precedence of that Corps.

4. Of being at Investitures of the Bath and the reception of addresses on the Throne on duty in the Throne Room and the only Guard there.

5. Of being at Coronations the Guard nearest to the Sovereign.

6. At the Lying in State of a Sovereign. Of being the only Guard on the platform with the Body, together with the Chief Mourners, Supporters, Heralds, &c.

7. Of attending Installations of the Garter.

Source: Brackenbury.

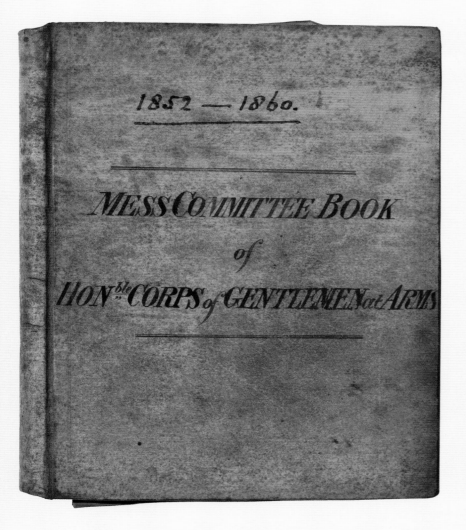

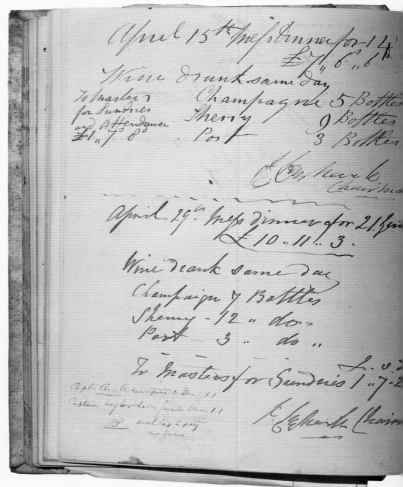

The Mess Account Book 1852-1860 gives an interesting insight into life as a Gentleman on duty in those days. Many small dinners were held in the Mess before and after duties in the 19th Century. The accounts suggest this was a lively time. April 14th 1856: Mess Dinner for 14: £7.6.6d. Wine drunk on the same day: Champagne 5 Bottles, Sherry 9 Bottles, Port 3 Bottles! The price for asking a guest was one guinea.

Through a Century of Wars to the Present Day

EDWARD VII – ELIZABETH II: 1901-2009

A busy Cold War era
Gentleman's coatee.
The six medals illustrated
(of his group of ten) are
from left to right:
Officer of the Order of the
British Empire
Campaign Service Medal 1962
with clasp 'Northern Ireland'
Gulf War 1990-91 with clasp
'16 Jan-28 Feb 1991'
Rhodesia Medal 1979-80
Accumulated Campaign
Service Medal
Service Medal, Order of St
John, which to this day bears
the head of Queen Victoria
The neck decoration is that
of a Commander of the
Order of St John.

The reign of King Edward VII, occupying, as it did, the first decade of the 20th century, saw the consolidation of the important reforms initiated by King William IV and executed by Lord Foley. It also saw, in its final year, the historic moment when the King, learning that his Nearest Guard had, since the Restoration, had a Standard Bearer but no Standard[36], presented them with one (see page 137).

Thus was the Body Guard's 400th year marked, a point at which this remembrancer must reluctantly leave go the hand of his invaluable predecessor, Major Henry Brackenbury, Gentleman at Arms: we can perhaps do no better than visit his final chapter.

After listing the Body Guard's early duties in the reign, recording that the 'Drawing Rooms' held in the previous reign at 2 o'clock in the afternoon became 'Courts' held at 10 pm, giving details of which Gentlemen did duty at the Coronation, postponed at the last minute due to the King's illness[37,] from a date in June to August 9th, 1902, Brackenbury concludes...

"His Majesty's Body Guard is now... as it was at its institution, a purely military body... There is happily little likelihood that this ancient Corps will be called on to show its devotion in an active manner, but should so improbable a contingency arise, it is animated with the spirit of its predecessors, and would strive to emulate their good deeds"[38].

Writing in 1905, during the *Belle Époque* of Galsworthy and Proust, Brackenbury gives us his own telling evocation of a world, a society and an age, unaware of impending, unimaginable, tragedy – war on a scale hitherto unknown.

left
King Edward VII (1841-1910)
by John Lewis Reilly.
Commissioned by King
Edward VII

above
On 14th May 1909 the
Gentlemen at Arms rehearsed
for the 400th Anniversary
Parade on the lawn at
Buckingham Palace. There
were 40 Gentlemen.
Photographs were distributed
to the newspapers, which

appeared the next day, even though the Parade was held in the picture Gallery. The Captain, Lord Denman commanded the parade, with drawn sword. Col Sir Henry Oldham, the Lieutenant, stands behind and to the right of Lord Denman. Col Sir Aubone Fife, the Standard Bearer is the nearest officer. He carried no Standard, since there was no Standard till later in the year. He served in the Defence of Canada 1866, with the Carabiniers in the Afghan War 1879-80, and seven frontier engagements before going on the Burmese Expedition in 1886; he was granted a 'step of honorary rank' for service in the field. The Clerk of the Cheque, Col Henry Fletcher, late Bengal Cavalry, stands on the right of the front rank. He served on the North West Frontier 1863-4, and was present at the action with the Mohmunds near Subkudder. He also served in the Egyptian War of 1882. The sub officer can be seen by the incorrect position of his sword scabbard, on the right flank of the rear rank. Captain Ernest Towse VC, the blind Gordon Highlander is on parade, but cannot be identified. (The Gentlemen did not plan to march past The King). Also on parade, but not identified, is Major Henry Brackenbury (61st Foot, a Goojerat 1848 veteran) who wrote the 1909 history.

The 1909 Standard.
Gold E VII R and Crown
Proper. Rose Shamrock and
Thistle Wreath, Proper.
Yellow tie to Wreath. Gold
Battle Axes, Gold Portcullis.
Crimson Damask Ground
and Pocket, Gold Fringe.
At the 400th Anniversary
Parade at Buckingham
Palace, King Edward VII
noted that there was no
Standard; a Standard Bearer
without a Standard seemed
curious. As part of the
Anniversary Celebrations it
was decided that henceforth
the Gentlemen should once
again have a Standard.
Confused stories about
Edgehill were largely
unproved, and medieval
pictures were regarded as
somewhat artistic. On 25th
June 1909 King Edward
presented a Standard to the
Corps in the Picture Gallery.
The King addressed the Corps:
*'It is only a few weeks ago that
I received you in this room, on
the occasion of the 400th
anniversary of your existence,
and the Corps at that time
was very anxious that I
should present them with
a Standard which they had
not carried since the reign
of King Charles I.
I am glad to have this*

*opportunity of presenting you
with a Standard, and its value
will be greatly enhanced by it
having been worked by the
wives and widows of former
Captains of the Corps…'*

The wives and widows of
former Captains who were
the donors of the Standard
and who worked some of the
embroidery were:-

H.R.H. The Princess Royal
Countess Beauchamp
The Lady Belper
Countess Carrington
Countess of Chesterfield
Countess of Coventry
Marchioness of Huntly
Dowager Countess of Rosslyn
Dowager Countess of
Shrewsbury
The Lady Sudeley
Countess of Yarborough
Lady Denman (wife of the
then Captain).

This Standard was in use till
1937, when following many
years of debate and study it
was agreed that its pattern
was wholly incorrect. It was
replaced by the correct style
now in use. The 1909
Standard remains in the
Orderly Room at St James's
Palace, loved by all for its
provenance and irregularity.

A Levée at St James's Palace by Messrs Dickinson, 1902-1905. Presumably painted for King Edward VII. The Gentlemen at Arms are clearly visible in the Queen Anne Room.

Four Gentlemen at Arms, with axes reversed, together with The Life Guards and Yeomen of the Guard stand vigil in Westminster Hall round the coffin of King Edward VII - , May 1910.

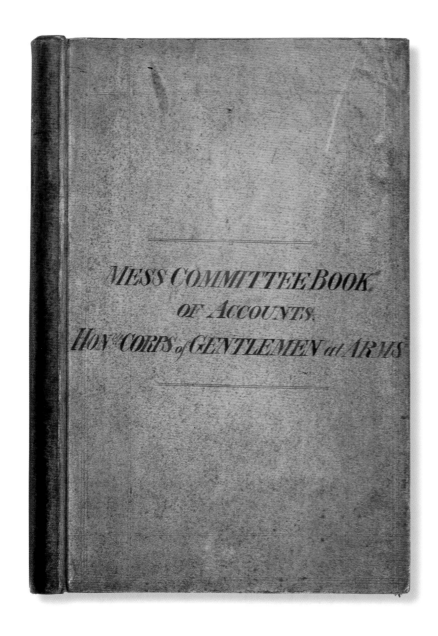

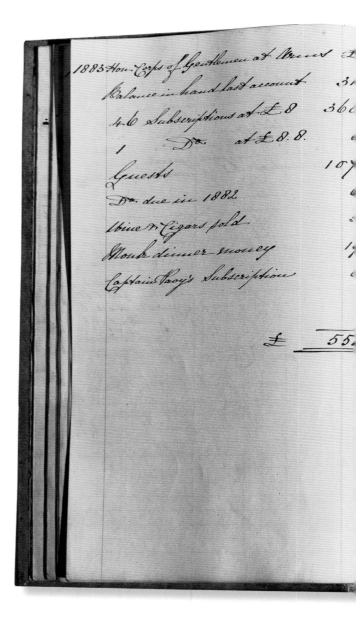

Mess Accounts for 1909 (the 400th Anniversary). Mess subscription £10.00 and joining fee 15 guineas. Subscription towards the 400 year anniversary banquet between 44 members £49.13.0. Catering, wine (from two suppliers) and printing costs are of interest.

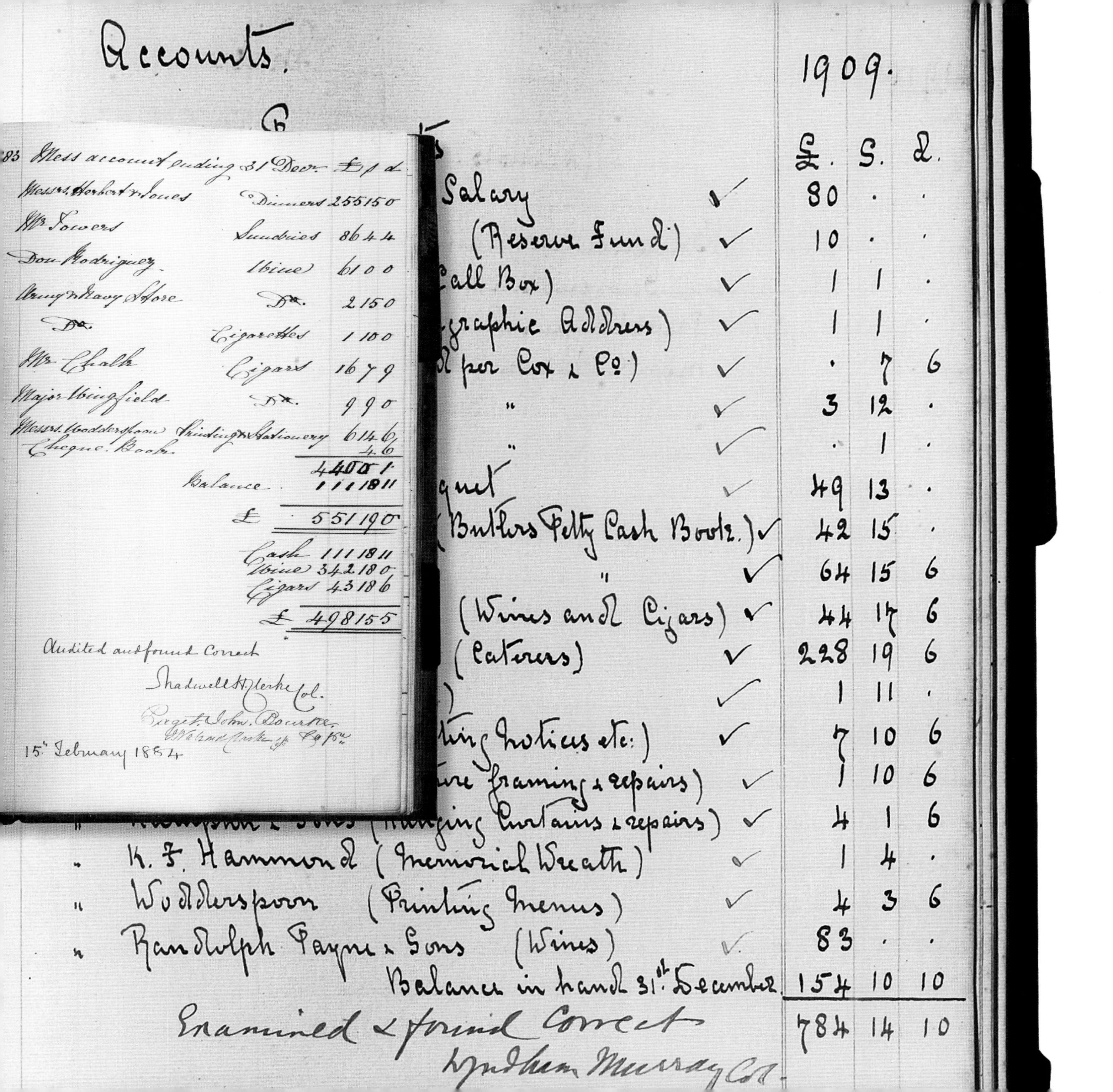

Left inset page

83 Mess account ending 31 Decr £ s d

Messrs Herbert & Jones	Dinners	255 15 0
Mr Towers	Sundries	86 4 4
Don Rodriguez	Wine	61 0 0
Army & Navy Store	D°	21 5 0
D°.	Cigarettes	1 10 0
Mr Chalk	Cigars	16 7 9
Major Wingfield	D°	9 9 0
Messrs Wodderspoon	Printing & Stationery	6 14 6
Cheque Book		4 6
		440 0 1
Balance		111 18 11
	£	551 19 0

Cash 111 18 11
Wine 342 18 0
Cigars 43 18 6
£ 498 15 5

Audited and found Correct

Shadwell H. Clerke Col.

Serjt. John Bourke
W. & A. Park & Co 15°

15 February 1884

Right page (1909)

		£	s	d
Salary	✓	80	.	.
(Reserve Fund)	✓	10	.	.
(Call Box)	✓	1	1	
(...graphic Address)	✓	1	1	
(... per Cox & C°)	✓	.	7	6
"	✓	3	12	.
"	✓	.	1	.
...quet	✓	49	13	.
(Butlers Petty Cash Book)	✓	42	15	.
"	✓	64	15	6
(Wines and Cigars)	✓	44	17	6
(Caterers)	✓	228	19	6
)	✓	1	11	.
...ting (notices etc:)	✓	7	10	6
...re (framing & repairs)	✓	1	10	6
...son & Sons (hanging Curtains & repairs)	✓	4	1	6
" K. F. Hammond (Memorial Wreath)	✓	1	4	.
" Wodderspoon (Printing Menus)	✓	4	3	6
" Randolph Payne & Sons (Wines)	✓	83	.	.
Balance in hand 31st December		154	10	10
Examined & found Correct		784	14	10

Wyndham Murray Col.

King George V (1865-1936)
by Richard Jack.

One of the earliest Duties of the Gentlemen in the following reign, on May 16th 1911, six weeks before King George V's coronation, was attendance at the unveiling of the Queen Victoria Memorial. Ordered by her son following her death, the massive structure, comprising some 2,500 tons of white marble, was still unfinished when *he* died, thus it fell to her grandson to inaugurate it.

Accompanied by his cousin, Kaiser Wilhelm II, who on the previous day had made a public declaration of their mutual friendship, the monument was duly unveiled. The King was so delighted with it that, taking a sword from his equerry, he knighted the sculptor, Thomas Brock, upon the spot.

It is perhaps a moment in our story at which to pause, and which to savour. At something of a hinge in history, a great reign and a great empire memorialised, two soon-to-be enemies in public amity, the occasion coloured and made specially memorable by an endearing act of royal spontaneity, the Body Guard was present, on duty, as ever at the heart of things.

Two contrasting entries for adjacent months in the Orderly Room Records[38] three years later illustrate the underlying realities of a society on the cusp and a world modulating to a tragic key...

"At the State Balls at Buckingham Palace on June 9th and July 16th, 1914, a Guard of ten Gentlemen at Arms, under the Clerk of the Cheque, was on duty to check disturbances by suffragettes...(and) ... In August, 1914, the Gentlemen still on Reserve (Major H.Schofield VC, Major F.Gascoigne DSO, and Major R.Webber) were recalled to the colours". The other Gentlemen, we learn, all "registered their names at the War Office for employment, and were gradually allotted appointments at home or abroad".

It cannot have been an easy recall for old soldiers, past the prime of life, whose previous active service had been in the Boer War, India, or elsewhere about the

left
The Unveiling of the Queen Victoria Memorial, 16 May 1911 painted by Sydney Pryor Hall. The Kaiser joins King George V to take the salute at the march past.

right
After the summer Coronation King George V and Queen Mary attended the Delhi Durbar in December 1911. It was perhaps the most spectacular and colourful ceremonial event in British Imperial history. Here the King Emperor arrives at the Selingarth Bastion. Two Gentlemen at Arms were on duty, without axes. They were (facing the camera) Lt Col W. Kenyon Mitford, 8th King's Royal Irish Hussars, who served in Afghanistan in 1879, and South Africa. HMBG 1900-1938. (Recalled for the Great War). The other Gentleman (Back to the camera) is Lt Col Mowbray Berkeley, late Black Watch who had already served on the Nile and in South Africa. He was recalled on the outbreak of War in 1914, and was killed in action 20th May 1916.

Empire. Indeed there surely can have been few times in history, if any, when weapons and tactics were so on the change: with manoeuvre replaced by trench-warfare, the machine-gun, wire and gas; the horse, eventually, ousted by the tank; the air even invaded. Was the old ever so starkly challenged by the new?

No criticism is intended of a man in that way much wronged, if we quote from then Major General Haig's *'Comments on the Training Season for 1913'* when he rebuked the Aldershot cavalry for failing to charge in the correct manner[39]. In spite of Lord Esher's reforms of the previous reign, we see an army apparently blind to the realities that were to face it twelve months hence.

Two Gentlemen were killed in action in France, Major Stewart MacDougall of Lunga, whilst commanding the 10th Battalion of the Gordon Highlanders, and Lieut-Colonel J. Mowbray Berkeley, while acting as a Camp Commandant: several were gazetted for various gallantry awards.

Among many memorable duties during the reign, the Corps was in attendance at the unveiling of the Cenotaph by the King, on November 11th, 1920; at the opening of the British Empire Exhibition at Wembley in 1924; at the funeral of Queen Alexandra in 1925; at the Silver Jubilee Thanksgiving Service at St Paul's Cathedral, and, finally, at the King's Lying in State and funeral in January 1936.

left

In 1919 the Gentlemen subscribed and bought a memorial to their comrades who died on service, or were killed in action during the Great War. The figure of Victory is that of the angel shown on the obverse of the 1914-1919 Victory Medal. The memorial which has been recently restored (2009), commemorates the following: Major Stewart MacDougall of Lunga, and Lt Col Thomas Mowbray Berkeley (who attended the Delhi Durbar in 1911). These Gentlemen are both pictured separately with a short biography. Lt Col Barrington Kennet and Capt the Hon Ivan Campbell died on active service.

1 9 2 4

right
The Gentleman at Arms in 1924 is depicted wearing a CMG, DSO the two South African War medals and the Great War trio, together with the Coronation Medals of 1902 and 1911. He had also served in the newly raised Territorial Army. This medal combination applied to several Gentlemen at that date, so he is hard to identify.

The abdication of King Edward VIII on December 11th 1936 brought to the throne, for the first time in seven reigns, a sovereign who had experienced active service, had seen war at first hand. The new King had served in the Grand Fleet, as a sub-lieutenant in HMS *Collingwood* at the Battle of Jutland in 1916. Posted to the Royal Naval Air Service, he went to Cranwell: Armistice Day found him in France, a flight lieutenant serving with the infant RAF. After the 'Great War', as it was at that time still hopefully known, he earned his pilot's wings.

These were to prove apt qualifications for shouldering the burdens that succession so unexpectedly thrust upon him: within less than three years of

Denis Fildes.

King George VI (1895-1952)
as Admiral of the Fleet by
Denis Quintin Fildes.
Presented to Queen
Elizabeth The Queen
Mother by the artist.

ascending the throne King George VI was to find himself at the head of a nation and an empire once again at war.

If, in 1939, the nation and the free world had yet to wait a year to find its voice, it had, in the King and his young family, exemplars of steadfastness and duty-before-self, proud to share with its citizens the privations and dangers of a London that was to become a target and a battlefield, and to endure unimaginable civilian casualties.

The Orderly Room holds eight volumes of the Body Guard's Order Books, the first initiated in 1830, when Lord Foley was Captain. Hand-written entries (how one regrets the demise of copper-plate and the advent of the blunt-nibbed fountain pen!) like annual rings, record the flux of the returning seasons of court duties year by year, as well as the names of all the Gentlemen who served with the Corps, with the dates of their enrolment, promotions, retirement and death.

The Order Books offer a taut note of contemporary events, as well as snatches of social history. We learn for instance that at the Opening of Parliament on October 26th 1937, for the first time, an "...omnibus conveyed the Gentlemen, who changed at Messrs Hawkes, from Savile Row (see pages 140-142) to the Victoria Tower... (another)... went straight to Chancellor's Court", that this was "a great convenience", and cost the Financial Secretary to the Household fifty shillings.

More notably, in June of that same, Coronation, year, a new Standard was presented by the King, replying to whose address, the Captain, Lord Lucan, reflected that the Body Guard's "duties now-a-days are not of such an active character as they were in the 16th Century". However, less than two years later, we learn of the Mess silver and plate being packed up for safe storage, and may read a memorandum from the Lord Chamberlain that released the Gentlemen from Household duties "to take on any appropriate war-work".

The response was exemplary, if no more than would be expected of such a body, and at such a time. The fifteen gentlemen still on the Reserve of Officers

Queen Elizabeth (later The Queen Mother) (1900-2002) by Sir Gerald Festus Kelly. Queen Elizabeth is depicted wearing her coronation robes. (Kelly enjoyed his sittings with the Queen and said of her, 'It is hard to suggest the admiration and affection which grew all around her. From wherever one looked at her, she looked nice: her face, her voice, her smile, her skin, her colouring - everything was right.')

between them wore the ribbons of no fewer than nine DSOs and eleven MCs on their return to full-time duty.

The 'war-work' of Colonel Sir John Lees DSO MC was commanding the 5th Battalion of his county regiment, the Dorsets, and that of Lieutenant Colonel Henry Houldsworth DSO MC, commanding the 4th Battalion Seaforth Highlanders in the 51st (Highland) Division. Let us for a moment break off to follow the latter through his second war with his two *Gazette* citations, for the DSO and bar.

The first, dated October 18th, 1940, reads *"Throughout the fighting for the Abbeville Bridgehead during the first week of June 1940... (he)... proved himself to be an outstanding Commanding Officer... his Battalion was detailed to take part in an attack on Mt de Caubert, in conjunction with French tanks.... (which... were) ... entirely destroyed ... shortly after crossing the starting line... (he) refused to admit failure, and by his personal example inspired his men to fight their way on towards the objective in spite of heavy casualties until he himself was wounded. His Battalion successfully held the ground they had gained until relieved after dark."*

Three years later, in the *Gazette* of October 14th, 1943, we read that, still with the 51st (Highland) Division, he *"commanded an Infantry Brigade throughout the Battle of Alamein in October and November, 1942, and during the subsequent advance up to Mersa Brega in December. Throughout that time he rendered most distinguished services and was an inspiration to his Brigade for his coolness under fire and his disregard of danger. (He)... never failed in action to visit the most forward troops of his Brigade, encouraging them by his unhurried movements, his thoroughness and his calm"*[40].

The war on the home front, which left over 50,000 dead, may be said to have started with the London Blitz on September 7th, 1940, and ended on March 27th, 1945 with the last V2 rocket. It was characterised, and is remembered by those who lived through it, as a time of blackout, sirens, shelters, sandbags, stirrup-pumps, gas-masks, ARP Wardens, Home Guard, rationing and evacuees.

If St James's fared better than twice-bombed Buckingham Palace, and a great deal better than the Palace of Westminster, it had several lucky escapes; nearby Jermyn Street was virtually levelled in mid-April 1941. On four separate occasions various of the Mess and Orderly Room windows were blown in.

With the suspension of the Body Guard's duties for the duration, the Axes, plate, office files and books were moved to safety in the cellar, and the two Standards sent to the strong room of the Army & Navy Stores.

Several organizations involved in war work were given use of the Engine Court premises, including the Lady Clerks of the Prisoners of War Services, and the Duke of Gloucester's Red Cross Fund. It was not until July of 1945 that the Axe Keeper, Mr Henry Harrison, was able to get the rooms in order again, and not until the last day of that month that the Clerk of the Cheque, Brigadier Kearsley, re-opened the Orderly Room[41].

The appalling losses when the Guards Chapel was hit by a flying bomb on Waterloo Day 1944, must have seemed very close to home for many of the Gentlemen, wherever they were serving at that time. But, let two memories of those proud, tragic, war years stand for all; they come, both, from November 1940.

The first is of our present Queen, aged fourteen, her sister beside her, broadcasting to the nation's children on the BBC. The other is of the scene at the Cenotaph, at the eleventh hour on the eleventh day. The Silence was broken by air-raid sirens: not a single person moved until the Reveille was sounded[42].

— —

The State Opening of Parliament in 1946 was the first post-war occasion when the Gentlemen fully returned to their court duties, the Order Books tell us. Almost exactly a year later, on November 20th, 1947, "the Corps was on duty in the Lantern and Choir at Westminster Abbey at the marriage of HRH The Princess Elizabeth to Lieutenant Philip Mountbatten KG RN (created Duke of Edinburgh on the eve of the wedding)".

State Opening of Parliament 1946. Field Marshal Viscount Alanbrooke (who carried the Crown in the procession) talking to Brigadier H Charrington DSO, MC*, and Lt Col C Carnegy . The Axe Keeper (1933-51), Mr Henry Harrison, complete with Bowler hat can be seen in the background. The Gentlemen at Arms had resumed their ceremonial uniform, while the Army in the post war austerity was still in service dress.

A summary of the Duties undertaken by the Corps in 1951, the last full year of the reign, gives an idea of those duties' frequency and scope:

"Presentation Parties – Buckingham Palace…13th & 14th March
Dedication Service Festival of Britain – St Paul's …. 3rd May
State Visit of TM The King & Queen of Denmark – Buckingham Palace… 8th May
Service of the Order of the Garter – Windsor……. 9th May
Presentation Party – Buckingham Palace …… 10th May
Service of the Order of the Bath – Westminster Abbey.. 24th May
State Visit of HM The King of Norway – Buckingham Palace….. 5th June
2 Garden Parties – Buckingham Palace… 12th & 19th July"

Of the Presentation Parties, it is noted, "For the first time the debutantes (without their mothers) went past and curtsied to Their Majesties".

Mourned by three Queens and by a nation that had yet to forget the unity of war, after struggling with ill health the King died, with unexpected suddenness,

State Opening of Parliament
1950. Left to Right: Col G.
Edwards DSO, MC (carrying
his head dress). Lt Col R.
Glynn MC. Col Lord Digby
DSO, MC, TD. Brig L Gibbs
CVO, DSO, MC*

in his sleep, at Sandringham, aged 56, on February 6th, 1952, whilst the Heir to the Throne was on a world tour.

More than three hundred thousand of his subjects paid their respects in Westminster Hall at the Lying in State, whilst the Body Guard carried out the penultimate Duty of the reign. The whole Corps shared the Duty, which ran from 3.30pm on Monday, February 11th, until 8am on the following Friday, a total of 88½ hours.

So ended the life of a much-loved king whose unlooked-for accession at a dangerous time had turned out to be so propitious for our monarchy, so affirmatory. A juncture that had at the outset seemed ill-starred, history shows to have been entirely fortunate. Throughout World War II, and in its austere aftermath, King George VI, his Queen, and their two daughters, were just what the country needed at its head, a family that ordinary people could look up to, yet identify with.

Came the moment: came the man.

———

Who that is old enough to have witnessed it can possibly forget June 2nd 1953? Certainly not the Sandhurst cadet who, of all the servicemen and servicewomen with duty on the processional route that day, was so lucky as to be posted at the junction of Tothill Street and Storey's Gate, straight opposite the west door of the Abbey.

He was among the first and closest of all the watching millions to see our young Queen, newly crowned, emerge onto the streets of her capital. It was indeed a time to remember... as was the sun-burst of optimism and hope that came with the start of a second Elizabethan reign.

The Order Book records of that great day that "The whole Corps, with the exception of the Lord Digby, who was summoned as a Peer, was on duty in Westminster Abbey. The Escort for HRH The Duke of Edinburgh was found by two Officers (the Standard Bearer and the Harbinger) and six Gentlemen, the six senior. The Escort for HM The Queen was found by two Officers (the Lieutenant and the Clerk of the Cheque) and twenty Gentlemen".

above

King George VI Funeral Feb 1952. Gentlemen at Arms, in great coats, with axes reversed, accompanying the gun carriage of HM King George VI to Paddington station, February 19.

right

Rehearsing for the Coronation service. 26 May 1953. Leaving Dean's Yard Westminster after the first rehearsal. (The axes were left at Westminster Abbey, hence the Gentlemen marching away with their umbrellas). A further rehearsal was held on 29th May, in morning dress complete with top hats for the aisle party. Top hats were worn for the procession up the aisle, and removed during the service (as were helmets on Coronation day, see the picture of the Coronation). Those on the first rehearsal were: Left: Brig R Daniell, Col Sir J Carew-Pole, Brig H Houldsworth, Col H Walsh, Maj Gen W Fox-Pitt, Maj Gen C Dunphie, Col Sir R Gooch. Right: Brig L Gibbs, Lt Col R Glynn, Lt Col Sir W Makins, Lt Col Hon O Vesey (Clerk of the Cheque).

If it is scarcely practicable to dwell in any detail on all the Duties and events that involved the Body Guard during the present reign, we might perhaps pause to take stock at the point at which the Corps completed the ninth half-century of its long history, in 1958. To mark the occasion the Queen, accompanied by the Duke of Edinburgh, honoured her Nearest Guard by dining with them.

If the Gentlemen seated at the mess table on that memorable evening, an occasion recorded by the artist Terence Cuneo, were different in almost every other way from the original Band of 'fiftie Speres', each with his 'archer, demi-launce, custrell and great horse', that accompanied their monarch at Guinegatte

The Coronation of Queen Elizabeth II, 2 June 1953 by Terence Cuneo (1907-96). Gentlemen can be seen on the right of the picture with their helmets on the floor. The Coronation picture took a year to complete and was presented to Her Majesty by her Lieutenants of Counties at a dinner at Lancaster House on 15 July 1954, when The Queen and The Duke of Edinburgh were entertained by the Lords Lieutenant of England, Scotland, Wales and Northern Ireland.

and the Siege of Boulogne, they were at least all battle-hardened warriors. They shared between the thirty-two of them a quite remarkable tally of gallantry awards, sixteen DSOs, two with bars, eleven MCs, seventeen Mentions-in-dispatches, two Croix de Guerre, and one US Legion of Merit with Silver Star[43].

The Captain in that landmark year was Major the Earl of St Albans; the Lieutenant, Lieut Colonel the Marquess of Ormonde MC; the Standard Bearer, Colonel Sir Bartle Edwards MC; the Clerk of the Cheque and Adjutant, Brigadier Sir Henry Floyd; the Harbinger, one of two Royal Marines on strength at that time, Major-General Arthur Chater DSO; and the Axe-Keeper, Mr Mark Smith.

Throughout the long reign that brings us to its Quinquennium Her Majesty's Body Guard of the Honourable Corps of Gentlemen at Arms, to give it for once its full title, continued its proud round of attendance on the Sovereign. Each year would see it on duty at Buckingham Palace, Windsor Castle, the Palace of Westminster, St Paul's Cathedral and Westminster Abbey, a routine leavened from time to time by Visits by Heads of State, and the high days of Royal Family and national celebration, Thanksgiving Services, Anniversaries and Jubilees.

For the first time in its history the Body Guard was on Duty at Caernarvon Castle, on July 1st, 1969, for the investiture of the Prince of Wales; at Coventry Cathedral, on May 25th, 1962, for its Consecration, and at Llandaff Cathedral, on June 14th, 1977, for a Silver Jubilee Service of Thanksgiving; and again, for the first time ever, in 2002, at the funeral of a royal centenarian, Queen Elizabeth, the Queen Mother.

Rare changes reflected changing times. Presenting Parties for debutantes were left off. When the Baroness Llewelyn-Davies received the Captain's Stick of Office at the Queen's hands in March of 1974, the Corps found itself with its first lady member, the first of two to date. The Queen directed that she should not wear the Body Guard's uniform, but a special badge, designed and made by the Crown Jewellers which is worn on a ribbon of the Corps colours.

The Queen and The Duke of
Edinburgh dine with the
Gentlemen at Arms on the
15th July 1965. Painted by
Terence Cuneo whose
trademark mouse is on the
small chest on the right.

1   Her Majesty Queen Elizabeth II

2   H.R.H. The Duke of Edinburgh

3   The Lord Shepherd

4   Brig. Sir Henry Floyd, Bt.

5   Lt.-Col. The Rt. Hon. Sir Michael Adeane

6   Lt.-Col. The Marquess of Ormonde

7   Lt.-Col. John Colvin

8   Lt.-Col. Hugh Hope

9   Major Derek Allhusen

10   Col. Samuel Enderby

11   Col. Ivo Reid

12   Col. Kenneth Savill

13   Col. Henry Clowes

14   Lt.-Col. George Kidston-Montgomerie
      of Southannan

15   Lt.-Col. Peter Clifton

16   Brig. Hon. Richard Hamilton-Russell

17   Col. Ferris St. George

18   Lt.-Col. Hon. Michael Edwardes

19   Brig. John Swetenham

20   Lt.-Col. John Robert Perry

21   Lt.-Col. John Chandos-Pole

22   Col. Sir John Carew Pole, Bt.

23   Brig. Robert Daniell

24   Brig. Anthony Pepys

25   Lt.-Col. Sir William Makins, Bt.

26   Col. Cecil Mitford-Slade

27   Brig. John Vandeleur

28   Lt.-Col. Frederick Lister

29   Major-Gen. Arthur Chater

30   Col. Sir Bartle Edwards

31   Col. Sir Robert Gooch, Bt.

32   The Dowager Duchess of Devonshire

33   Major-Gen. William Fox-Pitt

34   Lt.-Col. John Granville

35   Lt.-Col. Sir William Lowther, Bt.

36   Lt.-Col. William Heathcoat-Amory

37   Lt.-Col. Anthony Fulford

38   Brig. John Cheney

39   Lt.-Col. Kenneth Previté

40   The Axe-Keeper: Mr. M. C. Smith

41   Mr. S. Roblou

42   Mr. W. J. Watson

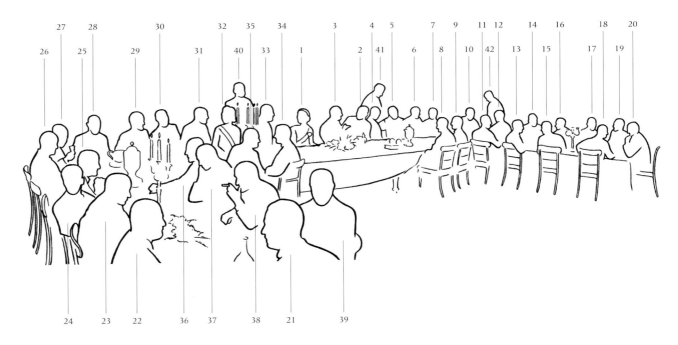

above

Gentlemen on duty accompanied by the first Lady Captain, Baroness Llewellyn Davies of Hastoe, and Officers of the Yeomen of the Guard at luncheon in the Chinese Dining Room at Buckingham Palace after the State Arrival of President and Senhora Geisel of Brazil on 4 May 1976. Officers of the Yeomen of the Guard (marked 'Y' in the list) can be identified by their double-breasted coatees, (two rows of buttons) with white facings (see the left hand standing officer) and their lack of a cross belt. Those present were:

Standing Left to Right: Col H Brassey (Y), Maj Lord Suffield, Lt Col M Edwardes, Maj D Dillon, Col A Way, Col C Pardoe, Col G Kidston-Montgomerie, Lt Col W Lithgow, Col I Reid, Col A Pemberton (Y), Lt Col D Laurie, Lt Col Sir W Lowther, Bt, Maj J Joicey.

Sitting, Left to Right: Col P Clifton, Lord Strabolgi (Captain of the Yeomen of the Guard), Baroness Llewelyn-Davies of Hastoe, Col K Savill, Col H Clowes, Lt Col J Chandos-Pole, Col S Enderby, Brig Hon R Hamilton-Russell, Lt Col R Perry, Brig J Swetenham, Lt Col Sir J Hornung (Y).
(There were at least seven DSOs and six Military Crosses, as well as a DSC and at least six OBEs or MBEs among those present on this occasion).

opposite page left

When Baroness Llewellyn Davies was appointed the first Lady Captain it was decided that Lady Captains should not wear uniform, but should carry the stick of office on formal parade occasions such as state arrivals. Her badge (referred to as such, and not as a brooch) was designed and produced by Garrard's the Crown Jewellers. Its safekeeping is the responsibility of the Lady Captain during her tenure of appointment. It is not allowed to be copied and must be handed in by an outgoing Lady Captain on the appointment of her successor and kept safe by the Lord Chamberlain's Office.

above right

1st July 1969, at Caernarfon Castle. In a ceremony with many historic echoes, directed largely by the Constable of the Castle, Lord Snowdon, The Queen invested The Prince with the Insignia of his Principality and Earldom of Chester: a sword, coronet, mantle, gold ring and gold rod. Six members of the Honourable Corps were on duty for the Investiture.

On July 9th, 1986, the Queen, accompanied by the Duke of Edinburgh, the Queen Mother, and the Duke of Kent, presented the Corps with a new Standard, in the garden of St James's Palace. After the event, and departing from the usual custom whereby correspondence between Buckingham and St James's Palace was conducted through the office of the Lord Chamberlain, Her Majesty sent a personal message of thanks to her Nearest Guard.

Coeval with the twentieth century, no consort in the history of our monarchy lived longer than did Queen Elizabeth the Queen Mother. Born on August 4th 1900, widowed on February 6th 1952, she died, aged 101, on March 30th, in Golden Jubilee year, 2002.

Her Majesty The Queen inspecting the Gentlemen at Arms in the garden of Clarence House on the occasion of the presentation of the new Standard, 9th July 1986. This was the first time in the existence of the Honourable Corps that there have been more than one Standard in a single reign, because there were no Standards in the long reigns of King George III or Queen Victoria. Lt Col R Mayfield DSO, Major M Colenso-Jones, Lt Col W Lithgow, Major T St Aubyn, Col Sir P Bengough KCVO OBE, Major M Drummond-Brady, Col D Fanshawe OBE. Behind The Queen Col R Crichton MC (The Lieutenant), The Lord Denham KBE (Captain). The Standard Bearer was Lt Col J Eagles.

The Queen and Prince Philip with the Gentlemen at Arms in 1993 at Buckingham Palace.

Seated: Brig A Breitmeyer (Harbinger), Lt Col Sir J. Scott (Standard Bearer), The Lord Hesketh (Captain). HM The Queen. HRH The Prince Philip. Lt Col T St Aubyn (Lieut), Col T Hall (Clerk of the Cheque). Standing Row 2: Lt Col J Fisher, Major C Gurney, Lt Col Hon N Crossley, Col J Baker, Capt the Lord Monteagle of Brandon, Lt Col R Mayfield, Col R ffrench Blake, Mr A Hayter (Axe Keeper, in Footman's uniform). Standing Row 3: Lt Col Hon G Norrie, Maj J Nunn, Lt Col B Lockhart, Maj M Colenso-Jones, Maj A Drummond-Brady, Lt Col R Macfarlane, Col T Wilson. Standing Row 4: Lt Col R Ker, Maj Sir P Duncombe Bt, Lt Col Hon P Lewis, Col Sir P Bengough, Maj JB Cockcroft, Maj R Nelson, Maj A Arkwright, Maj T Gooch. Standing Back Row: Maj I Ramsden, Maj Sir F Matheson of Matheson Bt, Col D Fanshawe, Maj P Johnson.

"The children won't leave without me. I won't leave without the King – and the King will never leave". Thus had she replied to Cabinet advice that she should move to Canada during the Blitz: thus is she remembered, especially by those who knew those times.

At the time of King George VI's death she caused to have sent a letter of thanks to the then Captain, Lord Fortescue, for the manner in which "The King's Nearest Guard" had carried themselves at his Lying in State and Funeral. One of their early duties in the new century, all but fifty years later, was attendance at her Funeral.

———

The day chosen to mark the Body Guard's 500th Anniversary, was Thursday, June 4th, 2009. Proceedings opened with a Service in the Queen's Chapel, a site so uniquely central to the history of the Monarchy, in which words and music rich in Tudor echoes (see page 146-147) were given memorable voice, and a sermon of rare weight and quality, celebrated the history and ethos of the Sovereign's Nearest Guard. The Bishop of London's text was St Paul's call to the Ephesians to "be strong" and "having done all, to stand".

The Service, an occasion never likely to be forgotten by those fortunate enough to witness or to take part in it, was followed by an equally memorable

In June 2002 Her Majesty The Queen celebrated her Golden Jubilee. A Review of veteran military bodies was held at Buckingham Palace. The parade was commanded by the Lieutenant of the Gentlemen at Arms. The parade consisted of The Military Knights of Windsor, The Yeomen of the Guard, The Royal Hospital Chelsea, The Band Yeomen Warders, and the Queen's Body Guard for Scotland, the Royal Company of Archers. *Front Rank (from this perspective):* Lt Col R. Ker MC, Maj O Howard, Lt Col J Fisher OBE, Brig R Dillon, Col Sir B Barttelot OBE, Maj the Hon N Crossley TD. *Rear Rank (from this perspective) right to left:* Col R ffrench Blake, Maj J Warren, Maj the Hon A Wigram MVO, (one invisible behind Lt Col Fisher), Col C MacKenzie -Beevor CBE, Maj Sir T Gooch Bt MBE (Standard Bearer with the Standard sloped for marching off), Col T Purdon OBE, Maj W Peto.

parade in Colour Court, a special programme of music (see page 146) being played by the bands of the Irish and Coldstream Guards, the latter in 18th century dress and with period instruments.

On the arrival of Her Majesty the Queen, accompanied by His Royal Highness Prince Philip, following the Royal Salute and Inspection, a Riband was blessed, and affixed to the Standard: the Queen then addressed her Nearest Guard....

"Captain Lord Bassam, Officers and Gentlemen, I congratulate you all on the occasion of the 500th anniversary of the establishment by King Henry VIII of what he envisaged should be 'a new and sumptuous Royal Guard'. The evils against which the Sovereign required protection in 1509 have I expect changed a little over the years but the loyalty of the Body Guard remains undimmed. As individuals, you have all given long and distinguished military service to the Nation. As members of the 'Nearest Guard', your service to the Crown continues in a distinctive way and reinforces the very best values of those who came before you.

It is more than twenty years since I presented you with the Standard paraded here. Today, I am pleased to have attached a commemorative Riband marking half a millennium of faithful service. I ask you to guard and honour it well in the tradition of your forebears and parade it with pride on the great occasions of State.

Prince Philip and I are delighted to be with you this morning and to wish the Honourable Corps of Gentlemen at Arms a long and prosperous future".

Thus the Sovereign's Nearest Guard entered on the sixth century of its long and honourable history.

"God Save the Queen".

The Quincentennial Parade

The 3rd Foot Guards mounting King's Guard in 1790 in Colour Court, St.James's Palace, where the Guard always mounted before Buckingham Palace became the principal residence in London for the Sovereign. This print shows the Guard marching exactly where the Gentlemen entered for the Five Hundredth Anniversary Parade. The Band wears uniforms like those of the Duke of York's Band of the Coldstream Guards in 2009.

Gentlemen marching in
single file into Colour Court
through the Great Gate on
the 4th June 2009.

page 132
The 'Duke of York's Band' of the Coldstream Guards with 18th Century uniforms and instruments.

page 133
The Regimental Band of the Irish Guards.

page 134
Major Charles Macfarlane. Uniform details on the Quincentennial Parade, 4th June 2009.

page 135
The Standard Bearer, Colonel Sir William Mahon, Bt.

page 136
The inspection, 500th Anniversary Parade.
left to right: Lt Col the Hon Guy Norrie (The Lieutenant), Col Christopher MacKenzie-Beevor CBE, HM The Queen, Maj Oliver Howard, Maj Charles Macfarlane, Maj Edward Crofton, Maj David Kennard, Lt Col Peter Browne MBE.

page 137
The Queen attaches the Commemorative Riband to the Standard assisted by The Lieutenant.

right
Quincentennial Celebrations 4th June 2009

Front Row - Seated: Col Robert ffrench Blake (The Harbinger), Col Sir William Mahon Bt (The Standard Bearer), The Lord Bassam (The Captain), HM The Queen, HRH The Duke of Edinburgh, Lt Col the Hon Guy Norrie (The Lieutenant), Lt Col Peter Chamberlin (The Clerk of the Cheque and Adjutant)
Row 2 - Standing: Maj Gen Jonathan Hall CB OBE, Maj William Peto, Col Edward Bolitho OBE, Col Robin Broke LVO, Maj John Rodwell, Maj Peter Johnson, Lt Col Peter Browne MBE, Maj David Kennard
Row 3 - Standing: Col the Rev Richard Whittington MBE, Maj Oliver Howard, Maj Charles Macfarlane, Col Michael Robertson MC, Major Michael Webster, Col Christopher MacKenzie-Beevor CBE
Row 4 - Standing: Maj Jeremy Warren, Col Peter Flach MBE, Maj Jeremy Russell, Lt Col John Fisher OBE, Maj Edward Crofton, Col Sir Charles Lowther Bt, Lt Col Rory Ingleby-MacKenzie, Brig Roger Dillon
Back Row - Standing: Maj the Hon Andrew Wigram MVO, Lt Col John Kaye, Col Sir Brian Barttelot Bt OBE, Col Timothy Purdon OBE, Lt Col Rhodri Traherne, Mr Pat Verdon (Axe Keeper)

Standard

Described by Brackenbury as 'debatable', the early history of the Body Guard's Standard is perhaps ground best left for experts to explore. This we do know, that there was a Standard Bearer from the very earliest days, that a Standard of various designs features in many of the depictions of battle and ceremonial scenes that survive, and that we need to be wary of confusing the Body Guard's Standard with the Royal Standard, as in the battles of the Civil War. However, three landmark occasions during the past century record the evolution of the Standard to its present happy, and we may safely say, final form.

The first of these occasions was in June of 1909, when, to mark the 400th anniversary of the Body Guard's foundation, King Edward VII presented a Standard that had been worked by the wives and widows of former Captains of the Corps under the supervision of the Princess Royal. We may draw our own conclusions from Kearsley's description of it as having "nothing to do with the original Standard of the Corps": writing in the same year, 1937, Crookshank tells us that the question of the correct Standard for the Corps had "been under serious discussion … and had been for some time a subject of great controversy". It seems that the well-intentioned efforts of the Buckingham Palace sewing bee had proved to be less than completely successful. Described by a later Standard Bearer as being "thoroughly nice but entirely wrong", it hangs today, amongst other treasures, in the Mess dining room.

The Standard presented by King George VI, on June 10th, 1937, which bore for the first time the Battle Honours of Guinegatte and Boulogne, did duty through that reign.

Its immediate replacement suffered an accident, being too vigorously flourished by the Standard Bearer, Major the Marquess of Donegall, catching on an axe, and tearing, at a State Opening. Invisibly mended by the wife of the then Lieutenant, Major David Jamieson VC, it also hangs, framed, in the dining room, behind the Captain's chair.

Her Majesty the Queen presented the present Standard, on July 9th, 1986. We give its Blazon below… *"In the first or chief place the Cross of St. George; in the second place the Royal Cypher ensigned with the Imperial*

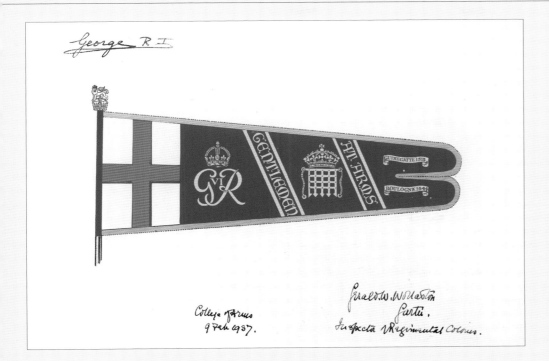

Crown proper; in the third place a portcullis chained and ensigned with a Royal Tudor Crown Or: and in the fourth place the two mottos also gold, the upper inscribed "Guinegatte 1513" and the lower "Boulogne 1544". Between four Bends across the flag the words "Gentlemen at Arms" all gold, the whole on a crimson field."

Sources: Brackenbury, Kearsley & Crookshank.

Uniform and the Savile Row Connection

The dress worn by the Body Guard went through many changes during the first three centuries of its history, from the strictly practical, if magnificent, 'battle dress' of Henry VIII's Pensioners, who were "apparelled and trapped in cloth of gold, silver, and goldsmith's work", to the pantomimic gear ordained for the Gentlemen at George IV's Coronation.

We may suppose that it was in reaction to this latter extravagance that the question of what uniform the Sovereign's Nearest Guard should wear began to be finally settled in the following reign, under the careful eye of a 'Sailor King', and the reforming Captain to whom so much is owed, Lord Foley. They wore the uniform of an officer of the foot-guards under King William IV, until, in the second year of Queen Victoria's reign, the present dress, that of a heavy Dragoon Guards officer, was decided upon.

The shako was abandoned for the helmet, ten years later, in 1848. On the order of the Earl of Tankerville, the plumes were regulated, "the length of the stem to be 9 inches, and the Feather 17 inches long" in 1867. On the order of Lord Coleville, today's pattern of sword, "The old Dragoon Guard Pattern 'Half Basket' hilt, Blade 36 inches long. Scabbard and Hilt – Steel or Silver-Plated" was adopted in 1919 (see page 33).

The Portcullis, the badge of the Corps, survives from the earliest days. Originally worn by the Beauforts in the Wars of the Roses, it was conferred on his Pensioners by King Henry VIII.

———

In the Body Guard's Quinquennial year it is happily exactly two centuries since Hawkes, who were the Duke of Wellington's tailor, were granted the Royal Warrant of Appointment to King George III. The firm had started, as velvet hat makers, in Brewer Street in 1771: Gieves, who dressed Nelson, originated in Portsmouth, fourteen years later.

Both firms were at the forefront of providing what their respective Services required on campaign or at sea. For instance, in 1809, Thomas Hawkes discovered the secret of 'jacking' leather to make it hard enough to withstand cuts from a sword blade, and invented the Shako, and later, the Hawkes Helmet or Solar Topee. In 1841, the firm that was to become Gieves, developed the prototype Sea Chest. The two firms became one, at No 1 Savile Row in 1974, thanks to an IRA bomb destroying Gieves's premises in Old Bond Street, thus merging the country's principal army and navy tailors.

1912 was the year in which Hawkes had moved to No 1 Savile Row, and in which they were appointed to dress the Gentlemen at Arms. As the Order Books in Engine Court record, it was in Coronation year, 1937, that an 'omnibus' was first

used to transport the Gentlemen from Savile Row to a Duty. We may perhaps assume that, from that year dates the present congenial practice of those Officers and Gentlemen of Her Majesty's Nearest Guard who are due for Duty gathering to dress on the first floor of the premises of Messrs Gieves & Hawkes, at No 1 Savile Row, and returning there, Duty done.

Sources: Brackenbury, Kearsley and Gieves & Hawkes 'Archive Guide'.

previous page
Col K Savill DSO leads the Gentlemen out of Messrs. Hawkes, at No 1 Savile Row where they changed into uniform prior to a duty. Gieves and Hawkes, after the happy amalgamation between the Wellington's tailor with Nelson's tailor continue to support the Gentlemen at Arms and look after their uniforms. The firm celebrated two hundred years of holding the Royal Warrant in 2009, and have supported this book.

this page (from left to right)
The Clerk of the Cheque's stick, like all the silver headed sticks, is engraved with the holder's appointment. The top of the silver head of the stick in each case bears the cypher of Queen Victoria.

The Harbinger carries an ivory headed stick of office, received from the hand of the Sovereign on appointment. Each officer also receives a commission on appointment from the Lord Chamberlain.

The Standard Bearer's stick which is carried on duties when the Standard is not on parade, such as the Evening Reception for the Diplomatic Corps, or in church.

The Captain carries a Gold Stick, which has a gold tassel, and like the other officers' sticks, is engraved with the holder's office. Lady Captains do not wear uniform, but are handed the stick of office by The Queen, and carry it when on duty in plain clothes.

The Lieutenant's stick.

The Ceremony of the Spurs

On the 4th June 2009, the Gentlemen wore uniform for the special 500th anniversary service in the Queen's chapel. Traditionally spurs may not be worn in the Chapel Royal without paying 'Spur Money' as this excerpt from the service shows. The choir boy was paid with a five pound coin specially struck to commemorate the Coronation of King Henry VIII. Each Gentleman was charged £5 on his Mess Bill, for the Choir Fund - to represent a penny for every year of the existence of the Honourable Corps.

A Gentleman-at-Arms is challenged by a Child of the Chapel Royal for wearing spurs.
Sub Dean (addressing the Lieutenant of the Gentleman at Arms) Sir, a Child of the Chapel Royal desires the honour of addressing you.
Child of the Chapel Royal
Sir, I perceive the wearing of Spurs within Her Majesty's Chapel Royal, and I therefore beg to request the payment of the customary Spur Money due thereon.
The Lieutenant of the Gentlemen at Arms
Boy, before acceding to your request, I require you to repeat the gamut.
Child of the Chapel Royal
Ut, re, mi, fa, so, la, si, ut
Whereupon the Lieutenant of the Gentleman at Arms shall pay to the Child of the Chapel Royal the customary fine.

The Corps Collect.
A special collect was written for the Five Hundredth Anniversary service by Colonel The Reverend Richard Whittington MBE, late Royal Engineers, a Gentleman at Arms, and the Chaplain of the Royal Hospital, Chelsea.

Music Awaiting the Arrival of The Queen and The Duke of Edinburgh

Medley 'Marching through the Centuries' arranged by Major P Shannon, MBE, Director of Music Irish Guards. This medley incorporates popular melodies which would have been well known on campaign by members of the Honourable Corps throughout the centuries. Tunes featured are:

Gathering Peascods. Composed by King Henry VIII.

Tallis Canon. Tallis was Organist and Composer of the Chapel Royal.

Lilibulero. 1600s. Sung at the Battle of the Boyne.

The Grenadiers March. The Seven Years War 1756-1763, and still used on The Queen's Birthday Parade.

Over the Hills and Far Away. 'Over the Hills and Over the Main, In Flanders, Portugal and Spain, Queen Anne commands and we Obey, O'er the hills and far away...'

See the Conquering Hero. Handel. March by the Court composer to King George III.

The Girl I left behind Me. The American War of Independence 1770s.

Garryowen. Very popular marching song over the centuries, especially in the Crimea and India at the time of the Indian Mutiny (1857), but really a much older air.

Boney was a Warrior. Napoleonic Wars; from an old Irish folk tune.

Soldiers of the Queen. Boer War 1899-1902 vintage. A Victorian patriotic popular song.

The Rakes of Mallow. A popular song for centuries and still used. Celebrates a surfeit of good living in the garrison in Limerick.

Rory O'More. Played by every band on duty at Queen Victoria's Coronation, and by The Life Guards Band as Queen Victoria returned to Buckingham Palace that day.

Capt EB Towse VC. In honour of the blind Gordon Highlander VC, a Gentleman at Arms who was on parade a hundred years ago. He was blinded in South Africa. Founder of the (Royal) National Institute for the Blind. Rejoined the Army, blind, in 1915, and typed letters for the wounded at Base Hospitals in France. MBE later CBE, later KCVO.

A Life on the Ocean Wave. For our two Royal Marines. There have been two Royal Marines in the Hon. Corps since the reign of King William IV.

Money Muntz. 1903 A Generic Cavalry march to satisfy our Cavalry Gentlemen!

Tipperary. The Great War 1914-1918.

White Cliffs of Dover/We'll Meet Again. Second World War.

Rule Britannia. Regimental March of The Royal Norfolk Regt. To celebrate the Normandy Campaign and the late Major David Jamieson VC, the last holder of that decoration to have served in the Honourable Corps.

Congratulations. 500 years.

To celebrate the occasion a new Corps March, entitled The Nearest Guard, composed by Major Philip Shannon, MBE, Director of Music, Irish Guards was played for the march off parade.

A selection of illustrious
Gentlemen taken from the
Bodyguard's archive

Lt Col T Mowbray Berkeley

1909– 1916
The Black Watch.

Brigadier General Basil T. Buckley

CB, CMG, CVO

1922–1940.
Standard Bearer 1940–1942
Northumberland Fusiliers

Gentleman at Arms 1909. Served the Nile 1882 and South Africa 1899–1902. Rejoined the colours and was killed in action 20th May 1916. Commemorated on the Angel statue in the Orderly Room.

Commissioned Feb 1895. Served in the Soudan in 1898 with 1st Northumberland Fusiliers under Kitchener. Present at the Battle of Khartoum. (British medal and Khedive's medal with clasp). Served South African War 1899-1901, Garrison Adjutant Ladybrand and as Adjutant 2nd Northumberland Fusiliers. Commandant of a Mounted Infantry Battalion April to Oct 1900. Took part in the advance to Kimberley and the actions at Belmont, Enslin, Modder River, Magersfontein and the Relief of Kimberley. His activities included operations in the Orange Free State at Paardeberg, Poplar Grove, Driefontein, Vet River and Zand River. He also fought in the Transvaal at Johannesburg, Diamond Hill and west of Pretoria at Zilikat's Nek. With his service in Cape Colony included he gained a mention in despatches, Brevet of Major and the Queen's South Africa Medal with seven clasps. Promoted Lt Col, 5 Oct 1914 as a staff officer in the War Office. Staff Officer to Kitchener, he drafted Kitchener's strategic objectives for the Dardanelles campaign.

Colonel Richard Crichton, MC
1966–1979
Coldstream Guards.

Captain Rt. Hon. The Lord Denman,
GCMG, KCVO
1907-1911
The Royal Scots.

Major Desmond Dillon, DSC
1971–1988
Royal Marines.

With the British Expeditionary Force, France, 1940. Acting Commanding Officer 1st Bn Coldstream Guards, Dunkirk. MC 1940. 3rd Bn Coldstream Guards, Middle East Land Forces, and Brigade Major 28 Brigade in Greece 1945. Mentioned in Despatches 1945.

Captain in 1909 for the Four Hundredth Anniversary. Served in the 2nd Battalion, 1894–1896 in India.

Served in HMS *Kenya*, a Second World War cruiser, decommissioned in 1959. Distinguished Service Cross (DSC) for services in the Korean War up to 9 July 1951, features in the book '*In Harm's Way*'.

Colonel Eric FitzGerald Dillon
CMG, DSO
1930–1946
The Royal Munster Fusiliers.

Major General Sir Charles Dunphie
CB, CBE, DSO
1952–1962
Royal Artillery.

Served South African War 1900–01 in Cape Colony and Orange River Colony with the Army Service Corps. Transferred to The Royal Munster Fusiliers 1908. Retreat from Mons, DSO Feb 1915. Numerous staff and operational appointments throughout the war. Chevalier Legion of Honour, Officer of the Order of Leopold, French and Belgian Croix de Guerre.

Born 1902. Osborne and Dartmouth, intended to join the Navy but re-introduced pre-Great War eyesight standards precluded this. To Woolwich; commissioned Royal Artillery 1921. India, pig-sticking and polo. Staff College 1935, and GSO2 1st Armoured Division 1939, fighting his first rearguard action with the BEF. Evacuated through Cherbourg. Mentioned in Despatches. 1941 appointed Commander 20th Armoured Brigade. Transferred to Command 26th Armoured Brigade at the critical German counter attack at the Kasserine Pass in Tunisia. The

courageous delaying rearguard action by this brigade saved a rout. CBE 1942. DSO 1943. Wounded. Appointed Assistant Chief of Staff US 2nd Corps. Friend of Gen George Patton. American Silver Star. retired, CB 1948. Joined Vickers eventually becoming Chairman. Knight Bachelor. 1959. Died 1999.

Colonel Algernon George Durand
CB, CIE
1902–1923
Central India Horse.

Lieutenant Colonel James Eagles, LVO
1967–1981
Standard Bearer for Presentation of New
Standard, 1988.
Royal Marines.

Author of '*Making of a Frontier: Five Years
Experience and Adventures in Gilgit, Hunza,
Nagar, Chitral and the Eastern Hindu Kush*'
(published 1900 Murray of London).
Kinsman of the Durand family of the
Durand Line dividing India and Afghanistan.
He served in the Afghan war 1878-80 with
the Khyber Field Force and in the Hunza
Nagaar Expedition (in the Kharakoram
mountains) 1891-2, in command of the force,
being severely wounded. His services were
acknowledged by the Government of India
he was Mentioned in Despatches and
awarded CB, with the Brevet of Lt Colonel.

Commissioned 1936. Served in Plymouth,
Chatham, Portsmouth Divisions, as well as
RM Depot Deal and HMS *Iron Duke* and HMS
Sussex. During WWII he was a member of No
1 Mobile Naval Base Defence Organisation
(MNBDO1) serving in Light and Heavy AA
Batteries, and in a RM Search-light Battery.
In 1st Heavy Anti-Aircraft Regiment RM (ex
MNBDO1), during the invasion of NW
Europe he provided AA defences of the
Scheldt estuary in the winter of 1944. The
Brigade recorded 483 V1 and 313 V2 (rocket)
incidents in one month. Units of the Brigade
also formed rescue squads to help civilians

buried in buildings wrecked by V1s and V2s.

The last air attack on Antwerp, on New
Year's Day 1945, was initially at low level
(500ft), when the Brigade shot down four
planes; around this time the V1 and V2
attacks intensified. The Brigade was relieved
in March 1945, moved to Ostend and took
over AA defence for Ostend and Calais.

He held many exacting appointments
after the war being rewarded by the post of
Fleet Intelligence Officer South Atlantic and
South America 1955-1957, as a Lt Colonel in
HMS *Afrikander*, the Simonstown Naval
Base in South Africa. He retired in May 1965.

Colonel Samuel Enderby
CVO, DSO, MC
1954–1976
Standard Bearer 1976–1977.

Brigadier Sir Henry Floyd Bt.
CB, CBE
1949–1957
Clerk of the Cheque 1957–1963.
Standard Bearer 1963–1966.
Lieutenant 1966–1968

Major General William Fox-Pitt
DSO, MVO, MC
1947–1961
Standard Bearer 1961–1963,
Lieutenant 1963–1966
Welsh Guards

The Royal Northumberland Fusiliers. Commissioned Feb 1928. MC for the recapture of Old Jerusalem in October 1938. DSO Italy London Gazette April 1944. Declined offer to be Lieutenant of the Gentlemen, (lived in Northumberland). CVO June 1977. Father of Major Charles Enderby, Lieutenant, The Yeomen of the Guard.

Joined Dec 1917.
ADC to Allenby in Egypt, 1925–6. Equerry to Duke of Gloucester. Partner in Christies. 1939 rejoined 15th/19th Hussars. France Sep 1939. At Dunkirk acting CO. Brigadier (GS) 8 Corps, Apr 43, Normandy, Belgium, Holland. CBE. Chief of Staff 8th Army Italy. CB and Legion of Merit.

One of the original officers who transferred in when the regiment was founded. A 1914 Mons man.

Colonel Sir Robert Gooch
Bt, KCVO, DSO
1950–1963
Clerk of the Cheque 1963–1967,
Standard Bearer 1967–1968,
Lieutenant 1968–1973
The Life Guards

Major John Joicey, MC
1973–1971
9th Lancers.

Brigadier General Sir (Robert) Harvey Kearsley, KCVO, CMG, DSO
1922–1935
Clerk of the Cheque 1935–1945.
Lieutenant 1945–1955.

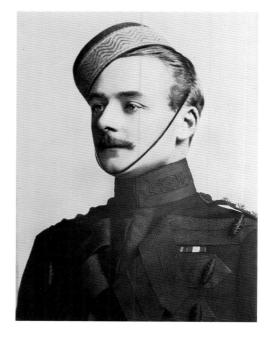

Commanded 1st Household Cavalry
Regiment Nov 1942–Dec 1944.
Despatches twice, DSO 1941.
Silver Stick 1944–1946.
KCVO 1973.
Son, Major Sir Timothy Gooch Bt MBE, also
Life Guards served as Standard Bearer 2002.

Also served in wartime 24th Lancers. MC
Italy. ADC to Field Marshal Lord Harding.
Resigned from the Gentlemen at Arms for
health reasons, and generously presented
the badged glasses to the Mess as well as a
photograph book.

Born 1880. Harrow. Author and prolific
archivist for the Gentlemen at Arms.
Served Boer War 1899–1902. 5th Dragoon
Guards Defence of Ladysmith and later
ADC to General RSS Baden-Powell (of
Scouts and Mafeking fame). DSO France
Feb 1915. Brigadier GS, Staff College 1919.
Uniquely he was an officer of the
Gentlemen at Arms at two Coronations.
Clerk of the Cheque for King George VI's
Coronation in May 1937 and Lieutenant for
Queen Elizabeth II's Coronation, June
1953. KCVO 1955.

Lieutenant Colonel William Lithgow

1970–1990
Royal Horse Artillery and 10th Royal
Hussars.

Lieutenant Colonel Sir William Lowther

Bt, OBE
1969–1982
8th, The King's Royal Irish Hussars.

Major Stewart MacDougall of Lunga

1900
Argyll & Sutherland Highlanders.

Fought as a Gunner officer in the Western
Desert, Sicily and Italy, went to India and
then the Army of Occupation of Japan.
After tours in the Canal Zone he
commanded The King's Troop, Royal Horse
Artillery and transferred the 10th Hussars
in 1961. He commanded in 1963 in
Germany and the Middle East in Aden. On
retirement he became Chef d'Equipe and
Chairman of Selectors for the highly
successful British Three Day Event Teams
in the Olympic and European Events.

Palestine 1936 (Mentioned in Despatches).
Prisoner of War from Western Desert till
1945. Commanded regiment in Korea,
(Mentioned in Despatches). Son, Col Sir
Charles Lowther, Bt, a Gentleman at Arms
from 1997.

Served with the Cameron Highlanders in
the Egyptian War of 1882, and was severely
wounded at the battle of Tel-el-Kebir.
Mentioned in Despatches, Medal with
clasp. Killed in Action 21st July 1915
Commemorated on the Angel Memorial in
the Orderly Room.

Major General Bertram Raveley Mitford
CB, CMG, DSO
1912–1936
The East Surrey Regiment.

Colonel W Kenyon Mitford
CMG, CVO
1900–1938
8th The King's Royal Irish Hussars.

Colonel Henry M. Pryce-Jones
CB, CVO, DSO, MC
1922–1938
Harbinger 1938–1949.
Standard Bearer 1949–1952.
Coldstream Guards.

Soudan Frontier Force 1886–88, Soudan Frontier, 1888–'9. Brigade Major under Kitchener 1896. Dongola Expeditionary Force. Khartoum. South Africa, Brigade major Mounted Infantry Division., Relief of Kimberley and numerous other actions. Five Mentions in Despatches before the Great War, DSO 1901. CB 1907. Retired 1910. Rejoined on outbreak of War 1914, Brigade commander 72 Brigade, Loos, Somme, Passchendale. CMG 1917. Major General 1918. Three Mentions in Despatches Great War.

Afghanistan 1879–1880, South Africa 1899–1902, Recalled to the First World War. Served the Crown 1879–1938, fifty nine years.

Served Boer War 1899–1902, Mentioned in Despatches. Advance to Kimberley, actions at Belmont, Modder River , Magersfontein etc. Queen's and King's South Africa Medals with 8 clasps. Served Great War MC June 1915. DSO June 1917. Five Mentions in Despatches. Second World War Secretary TA and Air Force Association, London, CB 1943. CVO 1952. Died Windsor Castle 1952.

Colonel Kenneth Savill
CVO, DSO
1955–1972
Standard Bearer 1972–1973.
Lieutenant 1973–1976
12th Royal Lancers

Colonel Ulric Thynne
CMG, CVO, DSO, TD
1922–1945
Standard Bearer 1945–1946.
The King's Royal Rifle Corps.
Later Colonel Wiltshire Yeomanry.

Commissioned in 1926 when the regiment was still horsed. Transferred to 1st The King's Dragoon Guards in 1936, in Secunderabad. In England on the outbreak of war, went to France as an intelligence officer with GHQ. During the period of the invasion scare of 1940–42, he attended the wartime staff course at Camberley, took part in raising the 27th Lancers and then commanded 161st Regiment RAC - a wartime armoured reconnaissance unit formed by a battalion of the Green Howards - before returning to the 12th Lancers as commanding officer in

November 1943 in Italy. Seven months of his command was in the infantry role, in the cold and mud of autumn in the Italian campaign. For the 12th Lancers' part in the hard fighting in November round Forli he was awarded the DSO. He was lucky not to be killed when a German sniper shot the driver of his jeep beside him. In 1947 he was appointed to command his third armoured regiment, the Queen's Bays (2nd Dragoon Guards), in the Canal Zone. Lived to age one hundred and one.

Chitral Relief Force 1895. South Africa with the Imperial Yeomanry, special service officer and Brigade Major Rhodesian Field Force (Mentioned in Despatches). DSO. Joined The King's Royal Rifle Corps at beginning of the Great War, serving in France and Belgium 1914–1918. (CMG 1918). Picture shows him as Colonel of the Wiltshire Yeomanry.

Colonel David Smiley LVO, OBE, MC*
1966–1968
Royal Horse Guards (The Blues).

A celebrated cloak-and-dagger agent of the Second World War with service behind the enemy lines in Albania, Greece, Abyssinia and Japanese controlled eastern Thailand, David Smiley was a sporting, unconventional officer of the Blues. He served in the Somaliland Camel Corps, the newly formed Commandos, SOE and his regiment. Among many other adventures he was at the capture of Tehran and commanded a Blues armoured car squadron at El Alamein. In Albania his speciality was bridge demolition, sometimes by climbing under them at night while German sentries were patrolling above. By this stage he had earned two Military Crosses. On Mountbatten's orders he re-armed Japanese and led them against the Viet-Minh in Indo-China. He took the surrender of Vientiane from a Japanese General. After the war he organised secret operations in Albania and Poland. This was followed, astonishingly, by command of the Blues at Windsor. He also commanded the Sultan of Oman's armed forces in the dramatic Djebel Akhdar campaign. With two squadrons of SAS under command he planned and led a brilliantly successful classic dawn attack on the 10,000 foot mountain. He retired from the Army in 1961, but he was soon in Yemen boosting the royalist forces, liaising with King Faisal of Saudi Arabia and MI6. It has been suggested that he was a model for James Bond. He was a man of true values and firm standards. Indeed, he commanded the Sovereign's Escort at The Queen's Coronation. Short though his time was in the Honourable Corps, he is looked upon with pride for his valiant service to his country.

Brigadier John (Joe) Vandeleur, DSO*
1953–1973
Irish Guards.

Colonel A.G Way, MC
1972–1988
Standard Bearer 1988-1990
Grenadier Guards.

Lieutenant Colonel Raymond Sudeley Webber
1914–1935
The Royal Welch Fusiliers.

Commissioned 1924. Served Sudan and Egypt before the Second World War. Commanding Officer 3rd Battalion Irish Guards which led the breakout of XXX Corps during Operation Market Garden to Nijmegen. Later commanded 129 and 32 Brigades. DSOs 31 Dec 1944 and 1 Mar 1945. Order of Orange Nassau. His role in 'A Bridge Too Far' was played by Michael Caine.

Commissioned 1939. Served in Tunisia 1942–43 as a company commander, and in Italy 1944. Awarded MC for leading No 1 Company in a battalion attack by 3rd Grenadiers for 1500 yards up Monte Grande on the night of 27–28 May 1944, personally commanding three local attacks on machine gun posts. Wounded by six bullets to the abdomen, he continued to give orders and control the battle. London Gazette 7 Dec 1944. Commanded 3rd Bn Grenadier Guards.

Burmese Expedition 1886-7. Dongola Expeditionary Force under Kitchener 1896 (with 12th Sudanese). Occupation of Crete 1898. South African War as ADC to Gen Rundle, (Severely wounded Mentioned in Despatches, Brevet of Major, Queen's and King's medals). His photograph shows twelve battle or campaign clasps.

HOLDERS OF THE VICTORIA CROSS

Note: In each case the period served with the Body Guard is shown in brackets.

Captain John Grant Malcolmson
(1870-1902)
3rd Bombay Light Cavalry
Battle of Koosh-ab, February 8th, 1857

Major James Leith
(1863-1869)
14th Hussars and Royal Scots Greys
Indian Mutiny, 1st April 1858.

Lt. Colonel Frederick Robertson Aikman
(1865-1888)
4th Bengal Native Infantry
Indian Mutiny, 1st March 1858

Major William Mordaunt Marsh Edwards
(1899-1912)
74th Regiment (Highland Light Infantry)
Tel-el-Kebir, 13th September 1882

**Major Alexander Edward Murray
(Viscount Fincastle), 8th Earl of
Dunmore** DSO MVO
(Captain 1924)
ADC Viceroy India attached to The
Guides Cavalry
Landakai, Tirah Campaign, India 17th
August 1897

Major Harry Norton Schofield
(1911-1931)
Royal Artillery
Colenso, 15th December 1899

Colonel Conwyn Mansel-Jones CMG DSO
(1920-1942)
The West Yorkshire Regiment
Terrace Hill, Tugela, 27th February 1900

Captain Sir Beachcroft Towse KCVO CBE
(1903-1920)
Gordon Highlanders
Magersfontein, 11th December 1899;
Mount Thaba 30th April 1900

**Major General Llewellyn Aleric Emelius
Price-Davies** CB CMG DSO
(1933-1948)
The King's Royal Rifle Corps
Blood River Poort, 17th September 1901

**Brigadier General Wallace Duffield
Wright** CB CMG DSO
(1932-1945)
The Queen's (Royal West Surrey) Regiment
Northern Nigeria, 26th February 1903

**Brigadier General George William St
George Grogan** CB CMG DSO
(1933-1945)
The Worcestershire Regiment
Bouleuse Ridge, Aisne, 27th – 27th April 1918.

**Brigadier General John Vaughan
Campbell** CMG DSO
(1934-1944)
Coldstream Guards
Ginchy, 15th September 1916

Major David Auldjo Jamieson CVO
(1968-1990)
The Royal Norfolk Regiment
River Orne, 7th – 8th August 1944

Sources: Kearsley; the Standard Bearer.

Captain Frederick Robertson AIKMAN,
VC, 4th Bengal Native Infantry
Indian Mutiny 1858 (Near Amethi, India)

Born Broomelton, Lanarkshire, 1828. Took part in the Sutlej Campaign of 1845-46, and also the Battle of Sobraon, receiving for his services at the latter a medal. He served throughout the Punjab Campaign of 1848-49 with General Wheeler's Field Force, receiving another medal. In the Indian Mutiny Campaign of 1857-58 he was present at the Siege and Capture of Delhi, at the action of Bolandshuhur and the Siege of Lucknow, and for his services received the Medal with two clasps, and was awarded the Victoria Cross (London Gazette 3 September 1858): *Frederick Robertson Aikman, Lieut, 4th Bengal Native Infantry. Date of Act of Bravery: 1 March 1858.* (Aged thirty). *This officer commanding the 3rd Sikh Cavalry on the advanced picquet, with one hundred of his men, having obtained information, just as the Force marched on 1 March 1858, of the proximity, three miles off the high road, of a body of five hundred rebel infantry, two hundred horse and guns, under Moosahib Ali Chuckbdar, attacked and utterly routed them, cutting up more than one hundred men, capturing two guns, and driving the survivors into and over the Goomtee.* (Darjeeling District of Bengal). *This feat was performed under every disadvantage of broken ground, and partially the flanking fire of an adjoining fort. Lieut.*

Aikman received a severe sabre-cut in the face in a personal encounter with the enemy.

This wound ultimately compelled him to retire on half pay.

Member of the Honourable Corps of Gentlemen at Arms from 13th May 1865 until his death on 5th October 1888.

According to the Times newspaper, he dropped dead while attending a ball.

Commandant for many years of the Royal East Middlesex Militia.

Buried at Kensal Green Cemetery.

(The 4th Bengal Native Infantry Regiment, being Bengali, was disarmed at Narpur and Hoshiarpore, which explains why Captain Aikman was commanding a Sikh Regiment during the Indian Mutiny Campaign, when he won his Victoria Cross).

Brigadier-General John Vaughan CAMPBELL, VC, CMG, DSO, ADC
Coldstream Guards. The Great War, Ginchy, France 15th September 1916

John Vaughan Campbell was the son of the Hon. Ronald Campbell, Coldstream officer killed on 28th March 1879 at Hlobane in the Zulu War performing an act of which General Sir Evelyn Wood VC said "I never saw a man play a more heroic part than he did yesterday." (The VC, however, could not then be awarded posthumously).

After education at Eton and Sandhurst he was commissioned in 3rd Battalion Coldstream Guards on 5th September 1896. He served numerous actions in the South African War from 1899 to 1902. He received the Queen's Medal with six clasps, the King's Medal with two clasps as well as two Mentions in Despatches and the *DSO. (London Gazette 27 September 1901): 'John Vaughan Campbell, Lieut. Coldstream Guards; In recognition of services in South Africa.'*

He was promoted Captain in 1903, and Major on 21st June 1913. He served in the European War from 1914 to 1918; temporary Lieutenant Colonel 29 July 1915, and Brevet 1st January 1916. He was awarded the Victoria Cross for his gallantry at Ginchy, France, 15th September 1916 (in the second long phase of the Battle of the Somme). *(London Gazette 26 Oct 1916): Major & Brevet Lieutenant Colonel (Temp Lieutenant Colonel) John Vaughan CAMPBELL, DSO 3rd Bn Coldstream Guards: For most conspicuous bravery and leading in an attack. Seeing that the first waves of his battalion had been decimated by machine gun and rifle fire he took personal command of the third line, rallied his men with the utmost gallantry, and led them against the enemy machine guns, capturing the guns and killing the personnel. Later in the day, after consultation with other unit commanders, he again rallied the survivors of this battalion, and at a critical moment led them through a very hostile fire barrage against the objective. He was one of the first to enter the enemy trench. His personal gallantry and initiative at a very critical moment turned the fortunes of the day and enabled his division to press on and capture objectives of the highest tactical importance.* Master of the Tanat Side Harriers (Shropshire), he rallied his men with his hunting horn, and subsequently became popularly known as the 'Tally Ho VC.'

CMG 1st January 1918. Commanded the 137th (Staffordshire) Brigade, 46th (North Midland) Division TF. The brigade was occupied for most of Campbell's command with the routine of trench holding, but on 29 September 1918 it spearheaded 46th Division's breaking of the Hindenburg Line at Belleglise, a brilliant feat of arms. Campbell's achievement was recognised five days before the war ended by his transfer to command of 3rd (Guards) Brigade. Four times Mentioned in Despatches in the Great War. ADC to The King 5th June 1919.

Major William Mordant EDWARDS, VC
The Highland Light Infantry

Gazetted Sub-Lieutenant (unattached) on 22nd march 1877, and joined the 74th Highlanders (later 2HLI) in 1877.

He served in the Straits Settlements and Hong Kong and in Egypt in 1882. For services in this last campaign he received the Tel-el-Kebir Medal and clasp, the Medjidie, and Victoria Cross. (London Gazette 13 Feb 1883).

'William Mordaunt Marsh Edwards, Lieut, 2nd Battn. The Highland Light Infantry. Date of Act of Bravery: 13 Sept 1882.

For conspicuous bravery displayed by him during the Battle of Tel-el-Kebir, on 13th September 1882 in leading a party of The Highland Light Infantry to storm a redoubt. Lieut Edwards who was in advance of his party, with great gallantry rushed alone into the battery, killed the artillery officer in charge, and was himself knocked down by a gunner with a rammer, and only rescued by the timely arrival of three men of his regiment'.

He served in India from 1884 to 1887, and was five years Adjutant of the 3rd Battn. Highland Light Infantry. Retired 1896.

Joined the Honourable Corps of Gentlemen at Arms on 19th February 1899.

Held the Coronation medals of King Edward VII and King George V. Present at the 400th Anniversary Parade. Died at Hardingham Hall 17 September 1912. Buried St George's Churchyard, Hardingham, Norfolk.

**Brigadier-General George William
St George GROGAN**, VC, CB, CMG, DSO*
The Worcestershire Regiment.

General Grogan was born on 1st September 1875 in Fife, educated at Haileybury, and first saw service with the West India Regiment in 1896. He served in Sierra Leone in 1898, and West Africa 1898-99. Captain in the Egyptian Army from 1902 till 1907. In January 1908 he joined The Worcestershire Regiment as a Captain. General Grogan's earlier service was of that varied nature which must appeal to all those who search for the old element of adventure in soldiering.

Lieut. Colonel Grogan commanded the 1st Battalion The Worcestershire Regiment in France in The Great War. CMG in 1916. His leadership culminated in the action, which was to win the Victoria Cross on the Bouleuse Ridge on 29th May 1918.

London Gazette 25 July 1918: 'For the most conspicuous bravery and leadership throughout three days of intense fighting. Brigadier General was, except for a few hours in command of the remnants of the infantry of a division and various attached troops. His actions during the whole battle can only be described as magnificent. The utter disregard for his personal safety, combined with sound practical ability which he displayed, materially helped to stay the onward thrust of the enemy masses. Throughout the third day of operations, a most critical day, he spent his time under artillery, trench mortar, rifle and machine gun fire, riding up and down the front line encouraging his troops, reorganizing those who had fallen into disorder, leading back into the line those who were beginning to retire, and setting such a wonderful example that he inspired with his enthusiasm not only his own men, but also the Allied troops who were alongside. As a result the line held and repeated enemy attacks were repulsed. He had one horse shot under him, but nevertheless continued on foot to encourage his men, until another horse was brought. He displayed throughout the highest valour, powers of command and leadership.'

Two days after gaining the VC he was awarded a Bar to his DSO.

Subsequently he commanded the 23rd Brigade. After the war from May until October 1919, he commanded 238 Infantry Brigade in the Force operating in North Russia, for which he was awarded the CB.

He later went to India to command the 3rd Battalion The Worcestershire Regiment. Finally, he commanded the 5th Brigade at Aldershot. Brigadier-General Grogan retired in 1926 and on 28th November 1933 became a member of the Honourable Corps of Gentlemen at Arms. He was A.D.C. to the King from 1920 to 1926.

He retired from the Honourable Corps in 1945.

Major David Auldjo JAMIESON, VC, CVO. The Royal Norfolk Regiment. Gentleman at Arms 1968–1981. Clerk of the Cheque 1981-1986. Lieutenant 1986–1990.
The Second World War, Normandy 1944.

Born in Westminster, on 1st October 1920, elder son of Sir Archibald Jamieson KBE MC, chairman of Vickers Armstrong. He was educated at Eton.

Captain David Jamieson won the Victoria Cross for the magnificent leadership and courage he displayed in the desperate battle for the bridgehead on the River Orne in Normandy, which had been gained in August 1944 by the men of The Royal Norfolk Regiment during the breakout after the D-Day landings. In a dangerous period, during which his company was repeatedly assaulted by overwhelmingly powerful German armoured forces, Jamieson kept a cool head and displayed resolve and tactical skills which, over a period of 36 hours, held the Norfolks' hard-won position and eventually repulsed the enemy's tanks.

Jamieson, then a captain, was in command of D Company of the 7th Battalion of the Royal Norfolk Regiment in the 59th Division during the crossing of the Orne south of Caen, which was initially successful enough for a bridge to be built and for some tanks to reinforce the bridgehead. On 7th August, 12th SS Panzer Division, which had been rushed over from the Canadian sector, launched three successive counter-attacks with the new and powerful Mk VI Tiger tanks

supported by Mk V Panthers, the brunt of which fell on D Company. Jamieson displayed outstanding resource and steadfastness during the four hours fighting which resulted in the Germans being repulsed by nightfall.

The German armour renewed its attacks next day. Two of the three tanks supporting Jamieson's company were destroyed and the outside telephone of the third would not work. In order to contact its commander, Jamieson left his slit-trench under close-range fire and climbed on to its turret in full view of the enemy. He was hit in the head and left arm, but when his wounds had been dressed, he refused to be evacuated. By this time all the other officers of the company had become casualties, so he continued to command until the last Germans were successfully driven off the position again several hours later. The Germans launched three more attacks that day on D Company, which Jamieson managed to defeat largely by skilled direction of artillery fire. By evening, when 12th SS Panzer Division finally gave up, the company position was largely intact and ringed with German dead and burnt-out tanks.

(London Gazette, 26 October 1944) River Orne, Grimbosq, France, 7 - 8 August 1944, Captain David Auldjo Jamieson, The Royal

Norfolk Regiment. "Captain Jamieson was in command of a Company of The Royal Norfolk Regiment which established a bridgehead over the River Orne, south of Grimbosq in Normandy. On 7th August 1944 the enemy made three counter-attacks which were repulsed with heavy losses. The last of these took place at 18:30 hours when a German Battle Group with Tiger and Panther tanks attacked and the brunt of the fighting fell on Captain Jamieson's Company. Continuous heavy fighting ensured for more than four hours until the enemy were driven off, after suffering severe casualties and the loss of three tanks and an armoured car accounted for by this Company. Throughout these actions, Captain Jamieson displayed outstanding courage and leadership, which had a decisive influence on the course of the battle and resulted in the defeat of these determined enemy attacks.

On the morning of 8th August, the enemy attacked with a fresh Battle Group and succeeded in penetrating the defences surrounding the Company on three sides. During this attack two of the three tanks in support of the Company were destroyed and Captain Jamieson left his trench under close range fire from enemy arms of all kinds and went over to direct the fire of the remaining tank, but as he could not get in touch with the commander of the tank by the outside telephone, he climbed upon it in full view of the enemy. During this period Captain Jamieson was wounded in the right eye and left forearm but when his wounds were dressed he refused to be evacuated. By this time all the other officers had become casualties so Captain Jamieson reorganised his Company, regardless of personal safety, walking amongst his men in full view of the enemy, as there was no cover.

The enemy counter-attacked the Company three more times during that day with infantry and tanks. Captain Jamieson continued in command, arranging for artillery support over his wireless and going out into the open on each occasion to encourage his men. By the evening the Germans had withdrawn, leaving a ring of dead and burnt out tanks round his position.

Throughout these thirty-six hours of bitter and close fighting, and despite the pain of his wounds, Captain Jamieson showed superb qualities of leadership and great personal bravery. There were times when the position appeared hopeless, but on each occasion it was restored by his coolness and determination. He personally was largely responsible for the holding of this important bridgehead over the River Orne and the repulse of seven German counter-attacks with great loss to the enemy." He remained in the Army till 1948. Major Jamieson joined the Honourable Corps of Gentlemen at Arms on 13th September 1968. He was Clerk of the Cheque and Adjutant for a long period, 1981-1986, and retired as Lieutenant, being awarded the CVO, in 1990.

David Jamieson died at his home in Burnham Market, Norfolk, on 5th May 2001 and is buried in Burnham Norton Cemetery.

(Brevet) Major James LEITH, VC
14th Light Dragoons
Indian Mutiny 1858

Third son of the late General Sir Alexander Leith KCB, of Freefield and Glenkendie, Aberdeenshire.

Born Glenkindie, Aberdeenshire, 26 May 1826. Played Cricket for England. Gazetted 14th Light Dragoons (later 14th Hussars, The King's) as Cornet 4 May 1849, and became Lieutenant 27 May 1853

He served in the Persian Expedition of 1857 with the 14th Hussars (Medal). Lieut Leith also took an active part in the suppression of the Mutiny at Aurangabad; served with the Malwa Field Force at the Siege and Capture of Dhal, and was present at the actions before Mundesore (wounded), in the Battle of Gooravia and Relief of Neemuch. He next served with the Central India Field Force under Sir Hugh Rose, and was present at the Siege and Capture of Rathghur, Relief of Saugor *(Later the Indian Cavalry School)* Capture of Gurrakota and pursuit across the Beas, forcing of the Muddenpore Pass, Siege and Capture of Jhansi, action of the Betwa, and all the affairs during the advance on Calpee. In recognition of his gallant services he was twice Mentioned in Despatches, received the Indian Mutiny Medal, and was given the Brevet of Major 20 July 1858, and was awarded the Victoria Cross (London Gazette 24 December 1858):

'James Leith, Lieut. (Now Brevet Major),

14th Light Dragoons (now of the 6th Dragoons). Date of Act of Bravery: 1 April 1858. For conspicuous bravery at Betwa on 1st April 1858, in having charged alone, and rescued Capt. Need of the same regiment, when surrounded by a large number of rebel infantry. (Despatch from Sir Hugh Henry Rose GCB 28 April 1858)

Major Leith was put on the half pay list on 31st December 1861 and retired in 1864.

He joined the Gentlemen at Arms on 5th May 1863, in the room of Charles James Cox. Died May 13, 1869, Marylebone, London (aged 42 years 352 days). Grave: Towie Churchyard, Towie.

Captain John Grant MALCOLMSON, vc
3rd Bombay Light Cavalry
(Later 33rd QVO Light Cavalry, now part of
the Poona Horse, Indian Army)
Persian Expedition 1857 (Battle of Khoosh-ab)

Born 1835 at Muchrach, Inverness-shire. He entered the 3rd Bombay Light Cavalry, served in the Persian War, and was present at the capture of Reshire and surrender of Bushire in the Persian War.

(London Gazette 3 Aug 1860).

'Arthur Thomas Moore, Lieut and Adjutant, and John Grant Malcolmson, Lieut 3rd Bombay Native Cavalry. Date of Acts of Bravery: 8 Feb 1857.

On the occasion of an attack on the enemy on 8th Feb. 1857, led by Lieut Colonel Forbes, CB, Lieut Moore the Adjutant of the Regiment, was perhaps the first of all by a horse's length. His horse leaped into the square and instantly fell dead, crushing down his rider and breaking his sword as he fell amid the broken ranks of the enemy. Lieut Moore speedily extricated himself, and attempted with his broken sword to force his way through the press; but would have assuredly have lost his life had not the gallant young Lieut Malcolmson, observing his peril, fought his way to his dismounted comrade through a crowd of enemies, to his rescue, and giving him his stirrup, safely carried him through everything out of the throng. The thoughtfulness for others, cool determination and ready activity shown in extreme danger by this young officer, Lieut Malcolmson, appear to have been most admirable, and to be worthy of the highest honour'.

He served in the Indian Mutiny Campaign of 1857-58, and was present at the Central India operations from the Siege of Ratghur to the fall of Calpe.

Joined the Honourable Corps of Gentlemen at Arms 27th May 1870.

Died at 29 Bramham Gardens, London on 14th August 1902 whilst still a member of the Honourable Corps.

Colonel Conwyn MANSEL-JONES
VC,CMG,DSO
The West Yorkshire Regiment.

Born 14 June 1871. Educated at Haileybury and The Royal Military College, Sandhurst.

Commissioned in The Prince of Wales's Own West Yorkshire Regiment, on 8th October 1890.

Served in the Ashanti Expedition of 1895-6 and in British Central Africa in 1898-99, and he took part in the Expedition against Quamba in August and September 1899, under the Foreign Office. He became captain on 20th March 1899.

On the outbreak of the South African War he rejoined his regiment in Natal, and was awarded the Regiment's first *Victoria Cross (London Gazette 27 July 1900): 'Conwyn Mansel-Jones, Capt., West Yorkshire Regt. On 27th February 1900, during the assault on Terrace Hill north of the Tugela, in Natal, the companies of the West Yorkshire regiment, on the northern slope of the hill met with a severe shell, Vickers-Maxim and rifle fire, and their advance was for a few minutes checked. Captain C. Mansel-Jones, however, by his strong initiative, restored confidence, and in spite of his falling very seriously wounded, the men took the whole ridge without further check; this officer's self-sacrificing devotion to duty at a critical moment having averted what might have proved a serious check to the whole assault'.*

He was engaged in recruiting from 1901, and was placed on retired pay in March 1910 on account of ill-health, caused by wounds.

On the outbreak of War in August 1914 he was mobilized and proceeded with the Expeditionary Force to France as DAAG General Headquarters (3rd Echelon), becoming AAG and temporary Lieutenant Colonel in December 1915. He served throughout the war in France. He was awarded the DSO on 3rd June 1915. In 1917 he was promoted to Lieutenant Colonel by brevet; and created Officer of the Legion of Honour by the President of the French Republic. In 1918 he was awarded the CMG, and he was six times Mentioned in Despatches.

He joined the Honourable Corps of Gentlemen at Arms on 10th December 1920, and died 29th May 1942. He is buried at Brockenhurst, Hampshire.

Major Alexander Edward MURRAY (Fincastle), 8th Earl of Dunmore VC, DSO, MVO.

The Captain 15th Feb 1924 - 5th Dec 1924

ADC to the Viceroy of India 1895-97. Sever Dongola Expedition 1896 (two medals). 1897 served with the Guides Cavalry in the Tirah Campaign in the Malakand Field Force, horse shot under him at Landakai. VC: *On 17 August 1897 at Nawa Kili, Upper Swat, India, Lieutenant Lord Fincastle with two other officers (Robert Bellew Adams and Hector Lachlan Stewart MacLean) and five men of the Guides, went under a heavy and close fire, to the rescue of a lieutenant of the Lancashire Fusiliers who was lying disabled by a bullet wound and surrounded by enemy swordsmen. Whilst the wounded officer was being brought under cover, he was unfortunately killed by a bullet. One of the officers of the rescue party was mortally wounded and four horses were shot.* Served with Buner Field Force (mention in Despatches, London Gazette 5 Nov 1897, 11 Jan and 22 April 1898). Served South Africa 1899-1902 with 6th Iniskilling Dragoons and 16th Lancers, and later raised 31st Battalion Imperial Yeomanry (Fincastle's Horse) in Scotland. Relief of Kimberley and numerous other operations till the end of the war. Queen's South Africa Medal with 4 clasps. Mentioned in Despatches (LG 10 Sep 1901). Served European War 1914, wounded DSO on the Somme. 4 Mentions in Despatches.

(Landakai: This action was part of Sir Bindon Blood's punitive measures, and is remembered for the heroism shown by a few members of the Guides cavalry.

Landaki is in the Swat Valley. The tribesmen had been driven from a spur of the mountains that had a narrow causeway running around it. The cavalry had to go along this causeway to chase the enemy in their retreat on the other side. The first two officers to reach the enemy were Lieutenant Palmer of the Guides and Lieutenant Greaves of the Lancashire Fusiliers. They were some way ahead of the rest and soon found themselves in trouble. Palmer was unhorsed and Greaves wounded. Colonel Adams and Lord Fincastle, an officer in the 16th Lancers, with two sowars managed to reach them as they were fending off sword blows. Fincastle's horse was killed and he tried to lift the wounded Greaves onto Adams's horse, during which Greaves received another bullet in the body and Adams's horse was wounded. The sowars rescued Palmer and took him to safety. Meanwhile, Lieutenant Hector Maclean and 4 sowars came to the help of the others. Maclean dismounted to get Greaves on to a horse and was shot dead in the process. Greaves, Adams and Fincastle managed to reach safety. The VC was awarded to Adams and Maclean of the Guides and to Lord Fincastle who was attached to the Guides, thus establishing a record three VCs won by a regiment in one day. The sowars received the Indian Order of Merit).

Major General Llewellyn PRICE-DAVIES
VC,CB,CMG,DSO
The King's Royal Rifle Corps.

Llewelyn Alberic Emilius Price-Davies, was born 30 June, 1878, third son of Lewis Richard Price, of Marrington Hall, Chirbury, Shropshire. He was educated at Marlborough and Sandhurst, and entered the Army 23 February 1898, serving throughout the South African War of 1899-1902. For his services in this campaign he was twice Mentioned in Despatches, received the Queen's Medal with five clasps, the King's Medal with two clasps, and was created a Companion of the Distinguished Service Order *(London Gazette,* 19 April, 1901*): "For services in South Africa".*

Price-Davies was awarded the Victoria Cross (*London Gazette*, 29 November 1901): *"Llewellyn Alberic Emilius Price-Davies, Lieutenant, King's Royal Rifle Corps. At Blood River Poort, on the 17th September 1901, when the Boers had overwhelmed the right of the British column, and some four hundred of them were galloping round the flank and rear of the guns, riding up to the drivers (who were trying to get the guns away) and calling upon them to surrender, Lieutenant Price-Davies, hearing an order to fire upon the charging Boers, at once drew his revolver and dashed in among them, firing at them in a most gallant and desperate attempt to rescue the guns. He was immediately shot and knocked off his horse, but was not mortally wounded, although he had ridden to what seemed to be almost certain death without a moment's hesitation".* He was promoted to

Captain 2 January 1902. In 1906 Captain Price-Davies married Eileen Geraldine Edith, daughter of James Wilson, DL, of Currygrane, Edgeworthstown, Ireland. From March, 1900 to July 1903, he was Adjutant and Quartermaster, Mounted Infantry, Irish Command, and from October 1906, to November 1907, was Adjutant, 5th Battalion Mounted Infantry, South Africa. He attended the Staff College, Camberley; and was Brigade Major, 13th Brigade, Irish Command from 1910 to 1912. He was then GSO3, War Office until 1914. From the outbreak of war on 5th August 1914 he was variously GSO3 2nd Division, GSO2 GHQ, GSO2 4th Division, until November 1915. Price-Davies was promoted Major 1st September 1915. He served in France from December 1915 to November 1917 (Brevet Lieutenant Colonel 1st January 1916). He then commanded a Brigade in England until 2nd April 1918; was created a CMG in January 1918; commanded a Brigade in France from the 3rd April 1918 to the 15th April, 1918, and was specially employed in Italy, with rank of temporary Major General, until the 31st December 1918; was given the Brevet of Colonel 3 June 1918.

Joined the Honourable Corps of Gentlemen at Arms in 1933, retiring in 1948. He died on 26 December 1965 in Corndon, Berkshire and was buried at Sonning.

Major Henry Norton SCHOFIELD
(DSO CANCELLED) VC
Royal Artillery South Africa, Colenso 1899

Harry Norton Schofield was born at Clayton, Lancashire on 29 January 1865, the son of a JP. Schofield passed out from the Royal Military Academy at Woolwich as a Lieutenant in the Royal Artillery in February 1884.

In 1899, during the Boer War campaign in South Africa, Schofield was Aide-de-camp to General Sir Redvers Buller, VC, GCB, GCMG, who commanded the Ladysmith Relief Force. (He had travelled to South Africa in the *Dunrottar Castle* with Sir Redvers Buller. A fellow-passenger was the young war correspondent Winston Churchill, who was taken prisoner by the Boers not far from the site of Schofield's heroic action at Colenso).

He was present at the Relief of Ladysmith, including the action at Colenso; at the operations of 17th to 24th January 1900, and the action at Spion Kop. Operations of 5th to 7th February 1900 and action at Vaal Krantz; operations on the Tugela Heights (14-27 February 1900) and action at Pieters hill. Operations in Natal (March to June 1900), including action at Laing's Nek (6-9 June 1900). Operations in the Transvaal, East of Pretoria (July to October 1900), including the action at Belfast (26 and 27 August 1900), and Lydenburg (5 to 8 September 1900).

At the Battle of Colenso General Buller had ordered Colonel Long to take two batteries of Field Artillery and six naval guns to support the main attack. The 14th and 66th Field Batteries of IV Brigade RFA were accompanied by six naval guns (two 4.7 inch and four 12-pounders) under Lieut Ogilvy of HMS *Terrible*. At an early stage in the action, Long's field guns unlimbered within a thousand yards of the enemy's trenches. From this position he opened fire upon Fort Wylie, which was the centre of that portion of the Boer line which faced him. The two batteries were without shelter of any sort, and in full view of the strongly entrenched and invisible enemy, and a fearful storm of bullets broke over them. After some time, owing to the ammunition running out, it was thought advisable to retire the officers and men to a small donga behind the guns, to which the wounded, including Colonel Long had been taken. About 800 yards to the rear of the guns was a deep donga or nullah, in which the drivers and teams were taking cover; along this Captain Schofield was riding with Sir Redvers Buller, who expressed a wish to try and get some of the guns away; so Gerard (the late Lord Gerard) and Schofield rode their horses into the donga and got some men and two teams out. Congreve, Schofield and Roberts, three aides-de-camp of the generals, were the leaders in this forlorn hope, the latter being the only son of Lord Roberts.

As soon as the teams were hooked in to the limbers on the bank of the donga, Captain Schofield gave the order to gallop for the guns, and as they got nearer, directed them on to the two on the right, as they appeared to be clear of dead horses. Corpl. Nurse galloped out with Schofield, and Roberts joined them, and was galloping along on Schofield's left. Congreve, after helping to hook a team in a limber, got his horse and came after them. On going about 400 yards, Roberts was shot and fell backwards. Congreve fell wounded when about 100 yards away from the guns, on reaching which, Capt. Schofield and Corpl. Nurse jumped off their horses and hooked in the two guns with which they returned. Captain Schofield sustained six bullet wounds in the action, The drivers, Henry Taylor, Young, Petts, Rockall, and Williams of the 66th Battery, all received the Distinguished Conduct Medal.

For his services in this campaign Capt Schofield was mentioned in Despatches (London Gazette 26 Jan 1900 and 8 Feb 1901; Sir Redvers Buller 30 Mar and 9 Nov 1900).

He received the Queen's Medal and with clasps, and was created a Companion of the **Distinguished Service Order (London Gazette 19 April 1901):** *'Harry Norton Schofield, Major, Royal Artillery: In recognition of services during the recent campaign in South Africa.'*

This distribution of awards was met with great consternation from the British public, since the press had fully acknowl-edged Schofield's successful and gallant action, and more importantly recognised him as the officer who had actually saved the guns. The public sympathy for Schofield was well illustrated in a letter from his stud groom, dated February 1900; *'I think it is a great shame you did not get the VC, perhaps you will get it yet. I hope you will. Everyone says you ought to have it. I am enclosing paper cuttings, which I thought you might like to see'.* General Buller justified his actions by stating "I have differentiated in my recommendations because I thought that a Victoria Cross required proof of initiative, something more in fact than mere obedience to orders". He concluded that Schofield, though courageous, had merely followed orders.

The award was cancelled nearly two years after the Battle of Colenso, when he was awarded the Victoria Cross instead of the DSO. (London Gazette 30 Aug 1901). *'The King has been graciously pleased to signify His intention to confer the decoration of the Victoria Cross upon the under mentioned officer, whose claims have been submitted for His Majesty's approval, for his conspicuous bravery in South Africa, as state against his name: Harry Norton Schofield, Captain, Royal Field Artillery. Date of Act of Bravery: at Colenso on the 15th December 1899. When the detachments serving the guns of the 14th and 66th Batteries, Royal Field Artillery, had all been killed wounded, or driven from them by* *infantry fire at close range, Capt. Schofield went out when the first attempt was made to extricate the guns, and assisted in withdrawing the two that were saved. Note. In consequence of the above, the appointment of this officer to the Distinguished Service Order which was notified in the London Gazette of 19th April 1901 is cancelled.'*

Captain Schofield was promoted to Major in 1900. As a Victoria Cross holder, Major Schofield was awarded the Coronation Medal 1902. He retired in December 1905. On 3rd May 1911 he became a member of the Honourable Corps of Gentlemen at Arms just in time for the Coronation of King George V on 22nd June 1911, for which he received the 1911 Coronation Medal.

Major Schofield was re-employed in the Great War 1914-1918, firstly on the British Remount Commission in Canada and America, and afterwards as Commandant on the Lines of Communication of the BEF. He retired in 1918 in the rank of Lieutenant Colonel.

He died on the 10th October 1931 in London and his funeral was held at the Chapel Royal at St James's Palace.

Lt Col Harry Schofield's Victoria Cross and medals are in Lord Ashcroft's collection. His Gentlemen at Arms helmet, complete with plume, was sold at auction by Wallis and Wallis of Lewes Sussex, in 1993, for £3,200.

Captain (Sir) Ernest Beachcroft Beckwith TOWSE VC, KCVO, CBE, The Gordon Highlanders.
South Africa. Two Actions 11th December 1899 and 30th April 1900.
(His Victoria Cross, unusually, has the two dates inscribed on the reverse).

Born 23 April 1864. Educated at Wellington College.

Gazetted to the Wiltshire Regiment 16 December 1885, and posted to the Gordon Highlanders 2 Jan 1886.

Served with the Chitral Relief Force 1895, including Malakand (Medal with Clasp). He also served on the North West Frontier of India and at Tirah, 1897-98 (two clasps) and with the Kimberley Relief Force in South Africa 1899-1900. London Gazette, 6th July, 1900

'Ernest Beachcroft Beckwith Towse, Captain, Gordon Highlanders. Date of Acts of Bravery: 11th December, 1899; 30th April, 1900. On the 11th April, 1899, at the action of Magersfontein, Captain Towse was brought to notice by his commanding officer for his gallantry and devotion in assisting the late Colonel Dowman, when mortally wounded, in the retirement, and endeavouring when close up to the front of the firing line, to carry Colonel Dowman on his back; but finding this not possible, Captain Towse supported him till joined by Colour-Sergeant Nelson and L/Corpl. Hodgson. On the 30th April, 1900, Captain Towse, with twelve men, took up a position on the top of Mount Thaba, far away from support. A force of about 150 Boers attempted to seize the same plateau, neither party appearing to see the other until they were but one hundred yards apart. Some of the Boers then got within forty yards of Captain Towse and his party and called on him to surrender. He at once caused his men to open fire, and remained firing himself until severely wounded (both eyes shattered), thus succeeding in driving off the Boers. The gallantry of this officer in vigorously attacking the enemy (for he not only fired, but charged forward) saved the situation; notwithstanding the numerical superiority of the Boers."

General Sir Horace Smith-Dorrien, (a survivor of Isandlwana 1879, and the hero of Le Cateau in 1914) recalled in his biography seeing Towse being carried down, blinded, from Mount Thaba; not a word about his terrible loss, he hoped that he had done his duty, and concerned about the survivors of his small detachment.

Captain Towse was decorated by Queen Victoria; she wept at seeing him, and awarded him a pension of £300 per year and in 1906 appointed Serjeant-at-Arms (The Investiture took place in the Throne Room of the State Apartments, St James's Palace). In 1902 he was re-appointed Serjeant-at-Arms by King Edward, and in 1903 became one of the Hon. Corps of Gentlemen at Arms. After the Great War he was appointed Serjeant-at-Arms in Ordinary to King George V.

Despite his blindness, returned to the colours during the First World War and became a well known figure at the base hospitals in France, where he used his skills as a typist to write letters for the wounded. He was mentioned In Sir Douglas Haig's Despatch of June 1916. He was rewarded with an MBE at the end of the war.

His military career behind him, Captain Towse turned his energies to the service of the blind community. In the years that followed he travelled the length and breadth of the country to help the British and Foreign Blind Association and foster public interest in the welfare of the blind.

The idea for the Fund was born in 1928 when Captain Towse received a visit from two close friends while on a long stay in hospital. Eager to help relieve the monotony of his hospitalisation, they rigged up a makeshift wireless set – earthed to a nearby radiator. This revelation transformed his life and inspired him to create the Fund.

The Fund was officially launched on Christmas Day 1929 by Winston Churchill (who had also been at Malakand on the Frontier) who broadcast an appeal, live, from his home in Chartwell with an impassioned appeal for money to buy wireless sets. In those days a reliable radio cost just £2 and fund volunteers would visit each recipient once a week to collect their radio batteries for recharging.

Whilst a Gentleman at Arms he fulfilled all the normal duties in uniform, being led to his post by the next for duty Gentleman. He was present at the 400th Anniversary Parade at Buckingham Palace.

Sir Beachcroft liked to be as independent as possible. Once when he was staying at a country house, his hostess decided to send her child up to his room to see if he needed help dressing for dinner. The child found him seated before the mirror at the dressing table, tying his white tie unconcernedly, in the pitch dark. "No thank you so much, I can manage very nicely!"

In 1920 he resigned from the Gentlemen at Arms and continued his work for the blind.

He died 21st June 1948 at Longmeadow, Goring-on-Thames, and is buried at St Thomas of Canterbury Church, Goring-on-Thames, Oxfordshire.

A (pipe) tune, re-arranged, named after him was played at the 500th anniversary.

Sir Beachcroft Towse's gold Body Guard tie pin is a proud possession of the Honourable Corps.

Brigadier-General Wallace Duffield WRIGHT

VC, CB, CMG, DSO, LEGION OF HONOUR
The Royal West Surrey Regiment
(The Queen's).
Northern Nigeria, March 1903.

Born in Gibraltar on 20th September 1875. He was commissioned into the 1st Battalion The Royal West Surrey Regiment (The Queen's) on 9th December 1896 and served with the Malakand Field Force and the Tirah Expeditionary Force 1897-1898. He became Lieutenant on 13th September 1898; Captain on 22nd January 1903; Brevet Lieutenant Colonel on 1st January 1916; and Brevet Colonel on 1st January 1919.

He passed through Staff College and was GSO 3 at the War Office from 2nd April 1909 to 15th August 1911, from 16th August 1911 to 1st April 1913 he was Brigade Major of the 3rd Brigade, Aldershot. On 28th January 1914 he was GSO 2 and employed with the West African Frontier Force, serving in the Cameroons. He served on the Western Front 1916-1919 with the Queen's Own Cameron Highlanders, and then as GSO 2 55th Division; GSO 1 18th Division; Brigadier General Staff of the 17th Army Corps and Brigadier-General in command of the 8th Infantry Brigade.

He was a member of HM's Body Guard of Honourable Corps of Gentlemen at Arms 1932-1945.

During the Second World War he served in the Home Guard.

He was awarded the CMG in 1916, the DSO in 1918; retired from the Army in September 1940, and was at one time a Member of Parliament. He died at Westways Farm, Chobham, Surrey, on 25th March 1953, aged 78.

He was decorated with the Victoria Cross by HM King Edward VII at Buckingham Palace on 5th November 1903.

His Citation reads:-

'On 24th March, 1903, Lieutenant Wright with only one officer and forty-four men took up a position in the path of the advancing enemy, and sustained the determined charges of 1,000 horse and 2,000 foot for two hours, and when the enemy, after heavy losses, fell back in good order, Lieutenant Wright continued to follow them till they were in full retreat. The personal example of this officer, as well as his skilful leadership, contributed largely to the brilliant success of this affair. He in no way infringed his orders by his daring initiative, as, though warned of the possibility of meeting large bodies of the enemy, he had purposely been left a free hand.'

Reference Section

Roll of Gentlemen

(p) = *Peninsular War*   *(w)* = *Waterloo*   *(c)* = *Crimean War*   *(m)* = *Indian Mutiny*

Surname	Christian Names	Rank	Year	Month	Regiment
Adamthwaite	George	Esq.	1828	May	
Agnew, MVO, DSO,	Quentin Graham Kinnaird	Major	1906	30 Apr	Manchester Regiment (DSO South Africa)
Aikman VC (M)	Frederick Robertson	Captain	1865	16 May	Bengal Army
Allhusen	Derek Swithin	Major	1963	26 Nov	9th Queen's Royal Lancers
Arkwright	Anthony Richard Frank	Major	1981	21 Oct	9th/12th Royal Lancers
Ashford	John	Esq.	1842	Apr	
Aubrey Fletcher, DSO, MVO	Henry Lancelot	Major	1936	21 Jul	Grenadier Guards (DSO 1918)
Bague	Charles	Esq.	1824	Nov	
Bague	George	Esq.	1825	Jul	
Baker	James Henry	Colonel	1988	15 May	Irish Guards
Barnard	Markland	Esq.	1851	May	
Barnett, CMG, DSO	George Henry	Lt Colonel	1926	02 Feb	King's Royal Rifle Corps
Barrington Kennett	Brackley Herbert	Lt Colonel	1895	20 Apr	King's Own Yorkshire Light Infantry
Barry, CMG, CBE, MVO, DSO	Stanley Leonard	Colonel	1923	05 May	10th Hussars
Barttelot, OBE	Sir Brian Walter de Stopham, Bt.	Colonel	1993	11 Sep	Coldstream Guards
Battye	Montagu John	Major	1875	13 Apr	Indian Army (QVO Corps of Guides)
Baynes	Charles Christopher	Esq.	1861	24 Jan	
Belcher	John Moulden	Esq.	1832	Sep	
Bengough, OBE	Piers Henry George	Colonel	1981	24 Jan	Royal Hussars
Bentley	Frederick Stocks	Esq.	1858	Nov	
Beresford	George de la Poer	Captain	1856	Feb	16th (Bedfordshire) Regiment of Foot
Berkeley	Thomas Mowbray	Lt Colonel	1909	23 Sep	Royal Highlanders (Black Watch)
Best *(m)*	Hon Frederick Barnwell	Captain	1867	18 Aug	2nd Bengal Fusiliers
Birkett	Frederick Blow	Esq.	1846	Feb	
Blackmore	Robert	Esq.	1835	Oct	
Blackmore	Robert	Esq.	1837	Jun	
Blake	Theobald	Esq.	1846	Feb	
Blakiston *(p)*	John	Major	1843	Dec	27th (Inniskilling) Regiment of Foot
Blenkarn	John	Esq.	1845	Feb	
Blewitt	Thomas	Lieutenant	1836	Aug	86th (Royal County Down) Regiment of Foot
Boggis Rolfe	James Edward	Captain	1861	17 Jul	55th (Westmorland) Regiment of Foot
Bolitho, OBE	Edward Thomas	Colonel	2008	15 Feb	Grenadier Guards
Bolton	Richard George	Captain	1856	Apr	5th (Princess Charlotte of Wales's) Dragoon Guards
Bolton	Augustus Samuel	Captain	1856	Feb	31st (Huntingdonshire) Regiment of Foot
Bourke	Paget John	Captain	1864	25 Apr	11th (North Devonshire) Regiment of Foot
Brackenbury *(c)*	Henry	Major	1877	09 Nov	61st (South Gloucestershire) Regiment of Foot
Breadalbane and Holland, MC	The Earl of	Lt Colonel	1935	23 Feb	Royal Artillery

In The Room Of	Remarks
Butler, Thomas	Resigned 1840
Gubbins, Charles E (Major) (Deceased)	Resigned 1936
Mills, Francis Vanderlure (Resigned)	Also Hon Colonel East Middlesex Militia. Died 1888
Houldsworth, Sir Henry, KBE, DSO, MC (Brigadier) (Deceased)	Promoted Standard Bearer 1981. CVO, Retired 9 Jan 1984
Jamieson, David A. (Major) VC Promoted Clerk of the Cheque	Promoted Standard Bearer 1999. Retired 2000
Hayward, Edward (Resigned)	Resigned 1848
Mitford, Bertram R. CB, CMG, SO. (Maj General) (Deceased)	Promoted Standard Bearer 1955. Died 1969. Author 'A History of the Foot Guards'
Busch, John	Resigned 1836
Smith, Edward	Resigned 1836
Way, Anthony G. MC. (Colonel) Promoted Standard Bearer	MBE 1999. Promoted Harbinger 2000. Standard Bearer 2003. Retired 15 Feb 2008
O'Kelly, Augustus de Pentheny (Resigned)	Resigned 1864
Home, Archibald F CB, CMG, DSO (Brig General) (Promoted Clerk of the Cheque)	Died 1942
Wyatt, Charles E (Major) (Half Pay)	Died 1919
Durand, Algernon G, CB, CIE (Colonel) (Resigned)	Died 1943
Nelson J Raymond E. (Major) (Resigned)	
Tyler, Charles. (Resigned)	Died 1894
Wise, William (Resigned)	The last Gentleman to purchase his place. Resigned 1869
Dakeyne, Thomas (Resigned)	Resigned 1838
Allhusen, Derek S. (Major). Promoted Standard Bearer	KCVO 1986. Promoted Standard Bearer 1997. Retired 22 Feb 1997
Robertson, Charles A L. (Resigned)	Resigned 1861
Hobson, Samuel (Captain) (Resigned)	Resigned 1857
Tufnell, Edward (Lt Colonel) (Deceased)	Killed in Action, France 1916
Bridge, George (Lt Colonel) (Resigned)	Resigned 1875
Murray, Charles Edward (Resigned)	Resigned 1849
Lonsdale, William (Resigned)	Resigned 1837
Bullock, William Daniel (Resigned)	Resigned 1839
Winter, Charles	Resigned 1850
Shakeshaft, Charles (Deceased)	Half pay 1865
Jones, Richard Nelson (Resigned)	Resigned 1846
Coxwell, Charles Rogers (Resigned)	Resigned 1844
Heyler, Francis John (Resigned)	Resigned 1869
Chamberlin, Peter, (Lt Colonel) Promoted Clerk of the Cheque	
Robertson, Henry (Resigned)	Resigned 1857
Jackson, Henry Augustus (Lt Colonel. Deceased	Resigned 1867
Vyvyan, Richard Henry S (Resigned)	Half Pay 1902
Dadson, William F P. (Captain) (Resigned)	
Pollen, Stephen H, CMG. (Lt Colonel) (Resigned)	Resigned 1938. Died 5 May 1959

Surname	Christian Names	Rank	Year	Month	Regiment
Breitmeyer	Alan Norman	Brigadier	1976	08 Aug	Grenadier Guards
Bridge	George	Captain	1854	Nov	3rd (East Kent The Buffs) Regiment of Foot
Broke, LVO	Robin George Straton	Colonel	1997	22 Feb	Royal Horse Artillery
Brooke Hunt	Robert Henry	Lt Colonel	1896	10 Feb	Seaforth Highlanders
Brown (m)	Edward	Hon. Colonel	1877	01 Jul	101st (1st Royal Munster Fusiliers) Regiment of Foot
Browne, MBE	Peter Dominick	Lt Colonel	2003	14 Jan	Royal Green Jackets
Buckley, CB, CMG	Basil Thorold	Brig General	1922	02 Jun	Northumberland Fusiliers
Buller (c)	James Hornby	Colonel	1881	22 Mar	The Military Train, Later 57th (West Middelsex) Regiment of Foo
Bullock	William Daniel	Esq.	1830	Mar	
Bullock	William Daniel	Esq.	1836	May	
Bunn	Alfred	Esq.	1836	Mar	
Burn (Forbes Leith)	C harles Rosen	Lt Colonel	1900	01 Dec	1st Dragoons
Butler, MC	The Lord James Arthur Norman, later Marquess of Ormonde	Lt Colonel	1936	03 Nov	17th/21st Lancers
Butts	Thomas	Esq.	1826	Mar	
Campbell	Hon Ivan	Captain	1901	20 May	Cameron Highlanders
Campbell, CIE, OBE	Charles Ferguson	Lt Colonel	1912	03 May	11th (PWO) Lancers (Probyn's Horse)
Campbell, VC CMG, DSO	John Vaughan	Brig General	1934	21 Feb	Coldstream Guards (DSO 1920)
Carew Pole, DSO, TD	Sir John Gawen, Bt.	Colonel	1950	29 Dec	Coldstream Guards
Cargill	William Walter	Esq.	1854	Jun	
Carleton, DSO	Frederick Montgomery	Brig General	1919	18 Mar	Royal Lancaster Regiment (The King's Own)
Carnegy, DSO, MC	Ughtred Elliott Carnegy (formerly Joseph)	Lt Colonel	1931	03 Oct	3rd Dragoon Guards (DSO & MC Great War)
Carver	Edward Furst	Esq.	1844	Mar	
Caulfield	Daniel	Captain	1832	Mar	17th (Leicestershire) Regiment of Foot
Chamberlain	Sir Henry Orlando Robert, Bt.	Lieutenant	1857	Oct	23rd (Royal Welch Fusiliers) Regiment of Foot
Chamberlin	Peter Guy	Lt Colonel	1993	15 Jun	Royal Green Jackets
Champion	Thomas Lyford	Esq.	1855	May	
Chandos Pole, OBE	John	Lt Colonel	1956	12 Oct	Coldstream Guards
Charnock	Richard	Esq.	1837	Jun	
Charrington, MC (DSO* WW2)	Harold Vincent Spencer	Colonel	1935	23 Feb	12th Lancers
Chater, CB, DSO, OBE	Arthur Reginald	Maj General	1949	16 Sep	Royal Marines
Cheney, OBE	John Norman	Brigadier	1948	03 Aug	King's Royal Rifle Corps
Chester Master, CB (m)	William	Brevet Colonel	1870	31 Oct	5th (or Northumberland Fusiliers) Regiment of Foot
Clarke	Edward	Esq.	1834	Nov	
Clarke	Henry Weller Ladbrooke	Esq.	1854	Nov	
Clarke (c)	John Walrond	Captain	1865	10 Mar	10th The Prince of Wales's Own Royal Hussars
Clement	Reynold Alleyne	Captain	1876	11 Apr	68th (Durham Light Infantry) Regiment of Foot
Clerke (c)	Shadwell Henry	Major	1875	16 Apr	21st (Royal North British Fusiliers) Regiment of Foot. (R Scots Fusiliers 1877)

In The Room Of	Remarks
Enderby, Samuel, DSO, MC. (Colonel) Promoted Standard Bearer	Promoted Harbinger 1992. Lieutenant 1993. Retired 14 Mar 1994
Watts, Francis (Deceased)	Resigned 1867
Bengough, Sir Piers KCVO, OBE. (Colonel) Promoted Standard Bearer	
Buller, James Hornby (Colonel) (Deceased)	Resigned 1920
Palliser, Arthur (Captain) (Resigned)	Half Pay 1903
Gurney, Carol (Major) Promoted Harbinger	
Rowley, Hon William C (Lt Colonel) (Resigned)	Promoted Standard Bearer 1946. Retired 1949. Died 16 May 1954
Dresing, Charles (Lt Colonel) (Half Pay)	Died 1896
Pitter, John (Resigned)	Resigned 1837
MacNeil, Hector Archibald (Resigned)	Resigned 1837
Bague, George (Resigned)	Resigned 1839
Chester Master, William, CB. (Colonel) (Half Pay)	Resigned 1929
Mexwell, Alexander G. OBE. (Lt Colonel) (Deceased)	Promoted Clerk of Cheque 1953. Lieutenant 1957. CVO 1960. Retired 25 Apr 1963
Sandys, Edwin	Resigned 1832
Holbech, Walter H (Lt Colonel) (Deceased)	Died on active service 1917
Murray, Sir Charles Wyndham, CB (Colonel) (Resigned)	Promoted 1922
Worgan, Rivers b CSI, CVO, DSO, (Brig General) (Deceased)	Died 1944
Wright, W D. VC, CB, CMG, DSO. (Brig General) (Retired 1945)	Promoted Standard Bearer 1968. Retired 4 Mar 1972. Died 26 Jan 1993
Hughes, William (Resigned)	Promoted Clerk of the Cheque 1856
Gore, George A E (Lt Colonel) Deceased)	Died 1922
Lauderdale, Earl of (Lt Colonel) (Deceased)	Assumed the name of Carnegy by deed poll 1915 on his mother succeeding to the estate of Lour, Forfar. Became Baron of Lour
Hamilton, Robert	Resigned 1845
Butts, Thomas (Resigned)	Resigned 1833
Beresford, George de la Poer (Captain) (Resigned)	Resigned 1860
Matheson of Matheson, Sir Fergus J, Bt. (Major) Promoted Standard Bearer.	Promoted Clerk of the Cheque 2008
Banks, John (Resigned)	Resigned 1857
Howard, Henry C L. CMG, DSO. (Colonel) (Deceased 1950)	Promoted Harbinger Feb 1966. Retired CVO 20 Jul 1979
Jones, William (Resigned)	Resigned 1841
Kearsley, R Hervey CMG, DSO. (Promoted Clerk of the Cheque)	Retired 19 Oct 1956. (DSO 1941 for service in Greece. Bar to DSO 1943 as Brigadier, 1st Armoured Brigade)
Lord Ellenborough, MC. (Major) (Deceased 1945)	Promoted Harbinger 1962. Retired CVO 7 Feb 1966. Died 3 Jan 1979
Barry, Stanley L. CMG, CBE, DSO, MVO (Colonel) (Deceased 1943)	Promoted Standard Bearer 1966. Retired CVO 1967. Died 13 May 1970
Messiter Sussex L A B. (Captain) (Deceased)	Half Pay 1900
Knapman, Edward (Resigned)	Resigned 1845
Hamilton, Frederick William (Resigned)	Resigned 1856
Harris, John Robin (Captain) (Resigned)	Half Pay 1900
Hume, Gustavus (Lt Colonel) (Promoted)	Resigned 1905
Best, Hon. Frederick B. (Resigned)	Died 1892

Surname	Christian Names	Rank	Year	Month	Regiment
Clifton, DSO	Peter Thomas	Lt Colonel	1960	03 Jun	Grenadier Guards
Clowes, DSO, OBE	Henry	Colonel	1961	31 Mar	Scots Guards
Cockcroft	Joh Barnaby Briggs	Major	1987	13 Oct	Welsh Guards
Cocum	John	Esq.	1824	Feb	
Colenso Jones	Gilmore Mervyn Boyce	Major	1982	26 May	Royal Welch Fusiliers
Collins	Arthur	Lt Colonel	1889	10 May	Middlesex Regiment
Colvin, OBE, MC	John Forrester	Lt Colonel	1945	18 Sep	9th Queen's Royal Lancers
Connor	William Hennry Brabazon	Esq.	1844	Nov	
Constable	George	Esq.	1839	May	
Cooch (c)	Charles	Colonel	1877	14 Mar	62nd (Wiltshire) Regiment of Foot
Cooke (p)	John Henry	Major	1844	Oct	21st Foot (Royal North British Fusiliers)
Cookney	James Wentworth	Esq.	1855	Jul	
Cotter	Sir James Laurence	Bt. Mil Rank not known	1850	Feb	27th (Inniskilling) Regiment of Foot
Cotton	George Finch	Esq.	1851	Jan	
Cox	Charles James	Captain	1851	Feb	Cinque Ports Militia
Coxwell	Charles Rogers	Esq.	1830	Mar	
Craster (c)	James Thomas	Major	1862	11 Aug	38th (1st Staffordshire) Regiment of Foot
Crichton, MC	Richard John Vesey	Colonel	1966	29 Jul	Coldstream Guards
Crofton	Edward Morgan	Major	1996	05 Jul	Coldstream Guards
Crookshank	Chichester de Windt	Colonel	1920	07 May	Royal Engineers
Crossley, TD	Hon Richard Nicholas	Colonel	1982	26 May	9th Queen's Royal Lancers
Culme Seymour	John Herbert	Lt Colonel	1883	23 Mar	82nd (Prince of Wales's Volunteers) Regiment of Foot. 1881: South Lancashire (PWV).
Cuninghame, DSO	William Wallace Smith	Lt Colonel	1936	21 Jul	Life Guards
Cunninghame C	William Cunninghame	Captain	1867	18 Aug	79th Regiment of Foot, or Queen's Own Cameron Highlanders
Curling	James Bunce	Esq.	1837	Sep	
Dadson (c)	William Frederick Portlock	Captain	1865	31 Oct	Royal Marines
Daly, MC	Victor Alexander Henry	Brevet Lt Colonel	1939	02 Jan	West Yorkshire Regiment
Dampier	Stephen Ryder	Captain	1856	Jul	Royal Aberdeenshire Highlanders.
Dance	David William	Esq.	1836	May	
Daniell, DSO	Robert Bramston Thesiger	Brigadier	1951	15 Jun	Royal Artillery
Daubeney	Frederick Sykes	Captain	1859	Mar	44th (East Essex) Regiment of Foot
Davidson	David William	Esq.	1836	Jul	
Davidson	Christopher Middlemas	Lt Colonel	1889	10 May	Royal Munster Fusiliers
Davies	Richard Edward	Esq.	1847	Mar	
De Blaquiere	Robert Milley	Esq.	1848	Apr	
Deane	Edward Pope	Esq.	1859	Feb	
Denne	George	Esq.	1844	Jan	

In The Room Of	Remarks
Chater, Arthur R, CB, DSO, OBE. (Maj General) Promoted Harbinger 1952	Promoted Clerk of the Cheque 1973. Standard Bearer 1979. CVO 1980. Retired 24 Jan 1981
Le Breton, Sir Edward P (Kt Bach 1941, MVO 1953) (Colonel) (Retired 1953)	Promoted Clerk of the Cheque 1967. Standard Bearer 1973. Lieutenant 1976 CVO 1977 KCVO 1981. Retired 21 Oct 1981. Died 8 Jan 1993
Steele, Robert, MBE. (Lt Colonel). Promoted Harbinger.	Promoted Clerk of the Cheque 1999. Lieutenant 2003. Retired LVO 2006
Wilkinson, Robert	Resigned 1831
Hope, Hugh, OBE, MC (Lt Colonel) (Deceased)	Promoted Harbinger 1997. Retired 2000
Aikman, Frederick R. (Lt Colonel) VC (Deceased)	Appointed Usher 1892. Died 1922
Smith, Herbert F E. DSO. (Died on active service 1940)	Retired 1965. Died 1980
Godden, John, (Resigned)	Resigned 1859
Bunn, Alfred (Resigned)	Resigned 1841
Lindam, Charles James (Major) (Resigned)	Half Pay 1911
Kincaid, John, (Deceased)	Promoted 1862 Exon (Yeomen)
Clarke, Henry Welller L. (Resigned)	Resigned 1862
Ford, Egerton (Resigned)	Promoted 1854. Appointment not clear
Lane, George (Resigned)	Resigned 1869
Ewart, Henry Larkins (Resigned)	Resigned 1863
Gardner, Philip Thomas (Resigned)	Resigned 1836
Jenkins, Thomas, (Major) (Resigned)	Resigned 1863
Heathcote Amory, William, DSO. (Lt Colonel) (Resigned)	Promoted Clerk of the Cheque 1979, Lieutenant 1981.CVO Retired 2 Oct 1986
Monteagle of Brandon, The Lord. (Captain) (Retired)	
Hume, Charles W (Major) (Deceased)	Retired 1943
Lowther, Sir W.Guy, Bt. OBE.(Colonel) (Deceased)	OBE 2001. Retired 2002
Nicholas, Griffen (Major) (Half Pay)	Promoted Clerk of the Cheque 1887
Agnew, Quentin DSO, MVO. (Colonel) (Resigned)	Retired 1959
Bolton, Augustus S (Captain) (Resigned)	Half Pay 1898
Harrison, William (Resigned)	Promoted Clerk of the Cheque 1838
Hunt, John Dutton (Captain) (Deceased)	Resigned 1877
Ricardo, Henry W R. CVO. (Major) (Retired)	Resigned 1951. (OBE 1945)
Marshall, William Julius (Resigned)	Resigned 1864
Bague, Charles (Resigned)	Resigned 1842
Grey, Clive O.V. CMG, DSO. (Lt Colonel). (Retired)	Retired 15 Oct 1971
Williams, Benjamin R. (Captain) (Resigned)	Resigned 1860
Layburn, John (Resigned)	Resigned 1838
Scott, Francis C. CB (Colonel) (Resigned)	Died 1922
MacNeil, Hector Archibald (Resigned)	Resigned 1856
Steele, William, (Resigned)	Resigned 1851
Connor, William H B. (Resigned)	Resigned 1861
Talman, Francis Henry (Resigned)	Resigned 1849

Surname	Christian Names	Rank	Year	Month	Regiment
Dick Cunynghame, CBE	Sir William, Bt.	Major	1920	10 Dec	Royal Highlanders (The Black Watch)
Digby, DSO,MC	The Lord, Edward Kenelm	Colonel	1939	18 Apr	Coldstream Guards
Dillon	Roger Edeveain	Brigadier	2002	22 Feb	Royal Marines
Dillon, CMG, DSO	Eric Fitzgerald (Viscount 1935)	Colonel	1930	21 Oct	Royal Munster Fusiliers (DSO Feb 1915)
Dillon, DSC	John Desmond	Major	1971	19 Oct	Royal Marines
Domville	William	Captain	1852	Apr	2nd or Queen's Royal Regiment of Foot
Doncaster	Harwick	Esq.	1856	May	
Dowling	Maurice	Esq.	1825	Nov	
Dresing	Charles	Captain	1861	22 Jul	3rd (East Kent The Buffs) Regiment of Foot
Drummond Brady	Michael John	Major	1981	15 Sep	The Queen's Regiment (Royal Sussex Regiment)
Dunbar *(c)(m)*	William Matthew	Lt Colonel	1882	16 Jun	24th (2nd Warwickshire) Foot. 1881: South Wales Borderers
Duncombe	Sir Philip Digby Pauncefort, Bt.	Major	1979	11 May	Grenadier Guards
Dunphie, CB, CBE, DSO	Charles Anderson Lane	Maj General	1952	13 May	Royal Artillery
Durand, CB,CIE	Algernon G A	Colonel	1902	01 Nov	Central India Horse
Dutton	William Holmes	Esq.	1832	May	
Eagles	Charles Edward James	Lt Colonel	1967	01 Dec	Royal Marines
Earle	Charles William	Captain	1866	14 Sep	Rifle Brigade
Edwards	Henry Herbert	Major	1892	18 Mar	Royal Welch Fusiliers
Edwards VC	William Mordaunt Marsh	Major	1899	19 Feb	Highland Light Infantry
Edwards, DSO, MC	Guy Janion	Colonel	1931	08 May	Coldstream Guards (DSO & MC Great War)
Edwards, MBE	Hon Michael George	Lt Colonel	1959	25 Dec	Rifle Brigade
Edwards, MC	Bartle Mordaunt Marsham	Brevet Colonel	1938	01 Jul	Rifle Brigade
Ellenborough, MC	The Lord	Major	1934	12 Jul	King's Own Yorkshire Light Infantry
Ellerthorpe	Jonathan	Esq.	1832	Aug	
Ellis	Francis	Esq.	1844	Jan	
Ellison *(c)*	Richard George	Major	1868	15 Feb	47th (Lancashire) Regiment of Foot
Enderby, DSO,MC	Samuel	Colonel	1954	07 Dec	Royal Northumberland Fusiliers
Ewart	Henry Larkins	Esq.	1837	Oct	
Ewart	John William Cheney	Esq.	1859	May	
Fairfax Ross, MC, TD	Thomas	Brigadier	1946	06 Aug	Rifle Brigade
Fanshawe, OBE	David Valentine	Colonel	1986	18 Apr	Grenadier Guards
Fergusson, CMG	William James Smyth	Colonel	1919	03 Jun	1st Dragoon Guards
ffrench Blake	Robert John William	Colonel	1990	01 Oct	13th/18th Royal Hussars (QMO)
Field	Aesculapius	Esq.	1838	Mar	
Fife	Aubone George	Lt Colonel	1887	30 May	6th Dragoon Guards (Carabiniers)
Fisher, OBE	John Howard	Lt Colonel	1990	05 Nov	Royal Marines (OBE Falkland Islands)
Flach, MBE	Peter Robert Cowley	Colonel	2006	27 Aug	Queen's Royal Hussars
Fletcher	Henry Arthur	Lt Colonel	1892	16 May	Indian Army
Floyd, CB, CBE	Sir Henry Robert Kincaird, Bt.	Brigadier	1949	30 Sep	15th/19th Hussars
Foote (MacDonald)	Gregory Grant	Esq.	1848	Nov	

In The Room Of	Remarks
Brooke Hunt, Robert H (Lt Colonel) (Resigned)	Died 1933
Fitzpatrick, Henry J. DSO. (Deceased)	Resigned 1962. (KG 1960. TD 1945)
Wilson, Timothy, (Colonel) (Retired)	
Stewart, Rupert. (Lt Colonel) (Deceased)	Died 1946 (Brigadier)
Daniell, Robert. DSO (Brigadier) (Retired)	Died 17 Oct 1988
Wright, Thomas George (Resigned)	Resigned 1860
Lamotte, John Lewis (Resigned)	Resigned 1869
Holl, Chase	Resigned 1831
Deane, Edward Pope, (Resigned)	Half Pay 1887
Joicey, John E. MC. (Major) (Deceased)	Retired 1999
Pavy, Francis (Captain), (Half Pay)	Half Pay 1890
Swetenham, John E. DSO (Brigadier) (Retired)	Promoted Harbinger 1993. Retired 18 May 1997
Wheatley, Leonard L. CMG, DSO. (Brig General) (Resigned 1946)	Resigned June 1962
Malcolmson, John Grant, VC, MVO (Captain) (Deceased)	Resigned 1923
Burton, Richard (Resigned)	Resigned 1833
Clowes, Henry, DSO, OBE (Colonel) Promoted Clerk of the Cheque	Promoted Harbinger 1981. Standard Bearer 1986. Retired LVO 15 May 1988
Winchester, George (Resigned)	Resigned 1870
Henry, Robert Edward, (Lt Colonel) (Deceased)	Died 1895
Noel, Edward Andrew (Colonel) (Deceased)	Died 1912
Waller, John H. CVO. (Captain) (Resigned)	Resigned 1951
Makgill Crichton Maitland, Mark E. CVO, DSO. (Lt Colonel) (Retired 1952)	Retired 29 July 1980. Died 12 Feb 1985
Pryce Jones, Henry DSO, MVO, MC (Colonel). Promoted Harbinger	Promoted Standard Bearer 1956. Knight Bachelor 1956. CVO 1961
Fergusson, William S. CMG. (Colonel) (Deceased)	Died 1945
Tyler, John (Deceased)	Resigned 1835
Smith, James Norton (Resigned)	Resigned 1845
Saunders, Henry F (Lt Colonel) (Resigned)	Appt Exon, Yeomen of the Guard 1884
Russell, Reginald E E. CVO, CBE, DSO. (Cvol) (Retired 1949)	Promoted Standard Bearer 1976. Retired CVO 1977
Weir, Hector Francis (Resigned)	Resigned 1851
Peto, James Fielder (Resigned)	Resigned 1864
Barnett, George H. CMG, DSO. (Lt Colonel) (Deceased 1942)	Died 1960
Pardoe, Philip. (Colonel) Promoted Harbinger	Promoted Clerk of the Cheque 1998. Lieutenant 2000. Retired LVO 2003
Barrington Kennett, B. (Lt Colonel) (Deceased)	Died 1934
Matheson of Matheson, Sir Torquhil, Bt (Major). Promoted Clerk of the Cheque	Promoted Harbinger 2006
Bull, John (Resigned)	Resigned 1859
Mortimer, Thomas B (Lt Colonel) (Half Pay)	Promoted 1891
Scott, Sir James, Bt. (Lt Colonel) Promoted Standard Bearer	Retired 20 Sep 2009
Mahon, Colonel Sir William, Bt. (Colonel) Promoted Clerk of the Cheque	
Collins, Arthur (Lt Colonel) (Resigned)	Promoted 1900
Thynne, Ulric O. CMG, DSO, TD (Lt Colonel) Promoted Standard Bearer	Promoted Clerk of the Cheque 1957, Standard Bearer 1963, Lieutenant 1966. Died 1968
Ashford, John (Resigned)	Resigned 1854

Surname	Christian Names	Rank	Year	Month	Regiment
Ford	Egerton	Esq.	1847	Mar	
Fox, OBE	Richard Simon	Colonel	1999	16 Nov	Queen's Royal Hussars
Fox Pitt, DSO, MVO, MC	William Augustus Fitz Gerald Lane	Major General	1947	12 Dec	Welsh Guards
Freme (c)	James Herbert	Captain	1865	28 Jul	79th Regiment of Foot, or Queen's Own Cameron Highlanders
Fulford	Francis Edgar Anthony	Lt Colonel	1948	03 Aug	Rifle Brigade
Gardiner	Philip Thomas	Esq.	1828	Dec	
Gascoigne, DSO	Earnest Frederick Orby	Major	1912	11 Oct	Grenadier Guards (DSO Egypt, Sudan and 'Khartum')
Gibbs, CVO, DSO, MC	Lancelot Merivale	Colonel	1939	02 Jan	Coldstream Guards (DSO & MC Great War)
Gibson	Robert	Esq.	1829	Mar	
Gifford (c)	John Wynter James	Captain	1875	19 Mar	3rd (Prince of Wales's) Dragoon Guards
Gilbertson	James Mattkins	Esq.	1842	Oct	
Glynn, MC	Rupert Trevor Wallace	Major	1939	02 Jan	Royal Artillery
Godden	John	Esq.	1838	Mar	
Gooch, DSO	Sir Robert Eric Sherlock, Bt.	Colonel	1950	21 Feb	Life Guards
Gooch, MBE	Timothy. (Sir Timothy Gooch Bt. from 1999)	Major	1986	02 Nov	Life Guards
Goodwin	Edward	Captain	1849	Jun	Cambridgeshire Militia
Gordon	John Henry	Esq.	1849	Nov	
Gore (m)	Charles Clitherow	Colonel	1887	27 Jan	Royal Irish Rifles
Gore	George Anthony Ellard	Lt Colonel	1895	01 Jun	Royal Marine Light Infantry
Gore, CB (CVO, CBE)	St.John Corbett	Colonel	1909	20 Aug	5th Dragoon Guards
Grace, MC	Humphrey Gilbert	Lt Colonel	1935	26 Jul	Probyn's Horse
Grange	Richard George	Captain	1852	Jun	Bengal Army
Grange	Robert	Captain	1854	Aug	Bengal Army
Granville (c) (m)	John	Lt Colonel	1962	12 Jun	Oxford and Buckinghamshire Light Infantry
Granville, DSO*	Bernard	Lt Colonel	1920	10 Dec	3rd (King's Own) Hussars (DSOs Great War)
Granvillle C	Bevil	Brevet Major	1863	09 Sep	23rd (Royal Welch Fusiliers) Regiment of Foot
Gray	Thomas	Esq.	1835	Dec	
Gray	Robert Alexander	Esq.	1837	Nov	
Gray, CMG, DSO	Clive Osric Vere	Lt Colonel	1932	21 Apr	Seaforth Highlanders
Green	David	Esq.	1845	Aug	
Gregory	John	Esq.	1843	Dec	
Gridley	Henry Gillet	Esq.	1860	Nov	
Grogan, VC, CB, CMG, DSO*	George William	Brig General	1933	28 Nov	Worcestershire Regiment (VC and 2 DSOs Great War)
Groves	Jeremy Grimble	Major	1997	26 Mar	17th/21st Lancers
Gubbins	Charles Edgeworth	Major	1897	01 Jan	Bengal Cavalry
Gurney	Carol James Hay	Major	1988	10 Oct	Royal Green Jackets
Hall, CB, OBE	Jonathan Michael Francis Cooper	Major General	1999	08 Mar	Royal Scots Dragoon Guards
Hall, OBE	Thomas Armitage	Colonel	1980	29 Jul	11th Hussars

In The Room Of	Remarks
Hoare, Edward Purefoy (Resigned)	Resigned 1850
Drummond Brady, Michael, (Major) (Retired)	Resigned 14 Sept 2000
Crookshank, CdeW, (Colonel) (Retired 1942)	Promoted Standard Bearer 1961.Lieutenant 1963, Retired CVO 1966. Died 1988
Blakiston, John (Major) (Half Pay)	Late Lt Colonel 1st Shropshire Rifle Volunteers. Resigned 1893
Campbell, John V. VC, CMG,DSO. (Colonel) (Deceased 1944)	Retired 23 Jul 1968
Blagg, William (Deceased)	Resigned 1830
Edwards, William M.M. VC (Major) (Deceased)	Promoted 1932
Mitford, W K. CMG, CVO (Colonel) (Retired)	Recalled to War Office to help with Victory Parade 1946. Retired 1959 (Brigadier)
Bulmer, William (Resigned)	Resigned 1833
Hampton, Thomas Lewis (Captain) (Resigned)	Died 1877
Walsh, Thomas George (Resigned)	Resigned 1849
Villiers, Charles H. CVO. (Major) (Retired)	Resigned 30 Oct 1961 (Lt Colonel)
Curling, James Bunce (Resigned)	Resigned 1844
Vivian, Valentine. CMG, DSO, MVO. (Lt Colonel)	Promoted Clerk of the Cheque 1963. Standard Bearer 1967. Lieutenant 1968
Promoted Clerk of the Cheque 1945	Retired KCVO.6 May 1973. Died 1978
St. Aubyn, Thomas E. (Major) Promoted Clerk of the Cheque	Promoted Standard Bearer 2000
	Resigned 2003. Died 9 Apr 2008
Maud, John George (Resigned)	Resigned 1885
Gilbertson, John Matthias (Resigned)	Resigned 1850
Culme Seymour John H (Lt Colonel) (Promoted [after less than 4 years service])	Resigned 1922
Morrison, John C D. (Colonel) (Half Pay)	Died 1914
Wingfield, Walter C. MVO. (Major) (Resigned)	Promoted Clerk of the Cheque 1920. 1920. Resigned as Lieutenant 1938. Died 1949
Scott, Lord Herbert M-D. CMG, DSO. (Lt Colonel) (Resigned)	Resigned 1950. Died 13 Feb 1953
Lyon, William (Resigned)	Resigned 1856
Tinkler, Wiliam Alexander (Resigned)	Resigned 1856
Dunphie, Charles A L. CB, CBE, DSO,(Major General) (Resigned)	Resigned 2 Jan 1970
Howard, Henry R L (Colonel) (Resigned)	Died 1933
Peters, James (Major) (Resigned)	Half Pay 1887. (Also Adjt Herts Rifle Volunteers)
Ellerthorpe, Jonathan (Resigned)	Resigned 1841
Knight, Joseph (Resigned)	Resigned 1841
Gascoigne, Sir Frederick, KCVO, CMG, DSO (Brig General) Promoted Harbinger	Died (while Hon. Mess Secretary) 3 Dec 1945
Clarke, Edward (Resigned)	Resigned 1850
Gray, Robert Alexander (Resigned)	Resigned 1845
Ewart, John William C (Resigned)	Resigned 1863
Granville, Bernard DSO (Lt Colonel) (Deceased).	Retired 1945. Died 1962
Nunn, Joshua A J. (Major) (Retired)	Died 2003
Somerset, Lord Edward (Major) (Resigned)	Died 1906
Rasch, Sir Richard C, Bt. (Major). (Retired)	Promoted Harbinger 2003. Retired 24 Nov 2006
Ramsden, Ivor, MBE. (Major). (Retired)	
Edwardes, Hon Michael, MBE. (Lt Colonel) (Retired)	Promoted Clerk of the Cheque 1993. Lieutenant 14 Mar 1994. Retired CVO 1997

Surname	Christian Names	Rank	Year	Month	Regiment
Hamilton	Robert	Esq.	1841	Apr	
Hamilton	Frederick William	Captain	1853	Jan	12th (Prince of Wales's Royal) Lancers
Hamilton Russell, DSO	Hon Richard Gustavus	Brigadier	1956	19 Oct	17th/21st Lancers
Hampton *(c)*	Thomas Lewis	Captain	1870	04 Mar	5th Dragoon Guards
Hanning	James	Esq.	1859	Feb	
Hardinge *(c)*	Henry	Lt Colonel	1863	05 Feb	Rifle Brigade
Harris	John Robin	Captain	1858	Jun	Kent Volunteers
Harrison	William	Esq.	1831	Sep	
Hay	Robert Bryce	Esq.	1849	Mar	
Hay	Robert Bryce	Esq.	1852	Apr	
Hayward	Edward	Esq.	1832	Oct	
Hayward	Edward	Esq.	1850	Apr	
Heathcote Amory, DSO	William	Lt Colonel	1950	29 Dec	King's Royal Rifle Corps
Helyer	Francis John	Esq.	1852	Apr	
Hemsley *(w)*	Henry	Lieutenant	1830	Oct	40th Foot (2nd Somersetshire)
Hennell	Reginald. DSO	Lt Colonel	1892	20 Feb	Bombay Infantry. (DSO Burma 1887. The DSO was instiued in 18
Henry *(m)*	Robert Edward	Brevet Lt Colonel	1869	20 Jul	20th (East Devonshire) Regiment of Foot
Hill	Augustus James	Lt Colonel	1891	17 Jul	Royal Marine Artillery
Hoare	Frederick Purefoy	Esq.	1844	Feb	
Hobson	Samuel	Captain	1853	Jan	10th (North Lincoln) Regiment of Foot
Hodgson	Henry Sibley	Esq.	1844	Jan	
Hodgson	Peter	Lt Colonel	1968	26 Nov	15th/19th Hussars
Holbech	Walter H	Colonel	1893	01 Jul	King's Royal Rifle Corps
Holloway	John Court	Esq.	1827	Aug	
Holmes	William Henry Muloch	Esq.	1846	Feb	
Home, CB, CMG, DSO	Archibald Fraser	Brig General	1919	04 Jul	11th Hussars
Hope, OBE, MC	Hugh	Lt Colonel	1963	25 Apr	King's Royal Rifle Corps
Hopkinson	Francis	Esq.	1838	Jan	
Hopton	Charles Edward	Captain	1856	Jan	23rd (Royal Welch Fusiliers) Regiment of Foot
Hornsby Drake	Alfred Western Hatchett	Lt Colonel	1895	20 Apr	1st Madras Lancers
Houldsworth, MC	Henry Walter	Lt Colonel	1939	25 Apr	Seaforth Highlanders
Howard	Thomas	Esq.	1850	Nov	
Howard	Oliver Crewdson	Major	2000	05 Jun	Royal Hussars (PWO)
Howard, CB	Henry Richard Lloyd	Colonel	1903	01 Jan	16th Lancers
Howard, CMG, DSO	Cecil Lloyd	Colonel	1935	07 Feb	16th Lancers
Hoy	Isaac Alexander	Esq.	1835	Jun	
Hughes	William Marjoribanks	Captain	1848	Jan	1st King's Dragoon Guards.
Hume *(c)*	Henry, CB	Colonel	1862	01 Dec	Grenadier Guards
Hume *(m)*	Charles Wheeler	Brevet Major	1888	09 Jan	Rifle Brigade
Hume *(c)(m)*	Gustavus	Lt Colonel	1872	13 Dec	38th (1st Staffordshire) Regiment of Foot

In The Room Of	Remarks
Matthews, James (Resigned)	Resigned 1844
Morison, James (Resigned)	Resigned 1854
Grace Humphrey G. MC. (Lt Colonel) (Resigned 1950)	Promoted Standard Bearer 1977. MVO 1977. Retired 4 Feb 1979
Earle, Charles William (Capt) (Resigned)	Resigned 1875
Hunter, John Alexander (Captain) (Resigned)	Resigned 1867
Craster, James Thomas (Major) (Resigned)	Resigned 1884
Salomons, Philip (Resigned)	Resigned 1865
Cocum, John (Resigned)	Resigned 1837
Tompkins, Benjamin (Resigned)	Resigned 1850
Lloyd, William, (Resigned)	Rejoined and Resigned 1852
Holloway, John Court (Resigned)	Resigned 1842
Thomson, James (Resigned)	Resigned 1859
Grogan, George W. VC, CB, CMG, DSO (Brig General) (Retired 1945)	Resigned 29 July 1966. Died 27 Aug 1982
Lloyd, Joseph Skipp. Promoted Clerk of the Cheque	Resigned 1861
Goter, William (Resigned)	Resigned 1837
Clerke, Shadwell H (Lt Colonel) (Deceased)	Apptd Exon, Yeomen of the Guard, 1894, Later Lieutenant, and Knighted 1902
Baynes, Charles C. (Resigned)	Died 1892
Fife, Aubone George (Lt Colonel) (Promoted)	Resigned 1914
Price, Francis Lysons (Resigned)	Resigned 1847
Roach, Richard Gates (Resigned)	Resigned 1856
Blewitt, Thomas (Lieutenant) (Resigned)	Resigned 1846
Carew Pole, Sir John, Bt., DSO, TD. (Colonel) Promoted Standard Bearer	Retired 23 Dec 1990
Freme, James H (Lt Colonel) (Resigned)	Died 1901
Mills, Benjamin	Resigned 1832
Trick, Frederick John (Resigned)	Resigned 1854
Hornsby Drake, AWH (Lt Colonel) (Resigned)	Promoted 1926
Gooch, Sir Robert E, Bt., DSO (Colonel) Promoted Clerk of the Cheque	Died 10 Apr 1982
Davidson, David William (Resigned)	Resigned 1843
Rice, George Watkin (Major) (Resigned)	Resigned 1858
Money, George N. CB. (Colonel) (Deceased)	Resigned 1919
Towse, Sir Beachcroft, VC, KCVO, CBE. (Captain) (Retired)	Died 1963. (DSO 1940 France. KBE 1960. Brigadier)
Wilkinson, George (Resigned)	Resigned 1871
Gooch, Sir Timothy, Bt., MBE (Major) Promoted Standard Bearer	
Stapleton Cotton, Charles MVO (Resigned)	Resigned 1920
Webber, Raymond S. (Lt Colonel) (Resigned)	Died 1950. CB.
Orme, Frederick Doveton (Resigned)	Resigned 1835
Walker, Tyrwhitt (Resigned)	Resigned 1854
Cooke, John Henry (Lt Colonel) (Resigned)	Appt Exon, Yeomen of the Guard 1873. Ensign 1889
Oldham, Henry Hugh (Colonel) (Promoted)	Died 1920
Taylor, William O'B. (Major) (Promoted)	Promoted 1876

Surname	Christian Names	Rank	Year	Month	Regiment
Hunter	John Alexander	Captain	1854	Nov	3rd (East Kent The Buffs) Regiment of Foot
Hunter	John Dutton	Captain	1857	Jun	Gloucester Volunteers.
Ingleby-MacKenzie, MBE	Roderick Alexander (Rory)	Lt Colonel	2007	25 Mar	Scots Guards
Jackson	Henry Augustus	Captain	1854	Nov	Regiment not recorded
Jamieson, VC	David Auldjo	Major	1968	13 Sep	Royal Norfolk Regiment
Jenkins	Thomas	Major	1861	29 Jul	Madras Army
Johnson	Peter David	Major	1990	23 Dec	Scots Guards
Johnston	Thomas Hayter	Esq.	1840	Jun	
Joicey, MC	John Edward	Major	1973	01 Jun	9th Queen's Royal Lancers
Jones	William Daniel	Esq.	1824	May	
Jones	Richard Nelson	Esq.	1838	Jan	
Kaye	John Robert Dennis	Lt Colonel	2003	02 Nov	King's Royal Hussars
Kearsley, CMG, DSO	Robert Harvey	Brig General	1922	15 Dec	5th Dragoon Guards (DSO France 1915)
Kelsey	Walter Frederick	Colonel	1890	01 Jan	Seaforth Highlanders
Kennard	Jeremy David	Major	2003	22 Apr	Irish Guards
Kenworthy	Edward Wilson	Captain	1852	May	Madras Army
Keppel	Edward George	Colonel	1894	17 Jul	Manchester Regiment
Ker, MC	Roger Hugh	Lt Colonel	1992	19 Jun	Royal Green Jackets (MC Northern Ireland)
Kidston Montgomerie of Southannon, DSO, MC	George Jardine	Lt Colonel	1956	14 Jun	4th Queen's Own Hussars
Killery	James	Esq.	1860	Nov	
Kincaid	John	Esq.	1839	Jul	
Kitson	George	Esq.	1846	Nov	
Knight	Joseph	Esq.	1829	Jan	
Lamotte	John Lewis	Esq.	1841	Oct	
Lane	John	Esq.	1849	Mar	
Lane	George	Esq.	1860	Nov	
Laurie, OBE,MC	David Alexander St George	Lt Colonel	1968	26 Mar	9th Queen's Royal Lancers
Le Breton	Edward Philip	Lt Colonel	1931	09 Jun	Royal Engineers
Lees, DSO,MC	Sir John Victor Elliott, Bt.	Lt Colonel	1938	25 Feb	King's Royal Rifle Corps
Leith VC	James	Major	1863	05 May	2nd Royal North British Dragoons (Scots Greys)
Lendrum	Rupert Charles Douglas	Major	2009	20 Sep	Blues & Royals
Lewis	Hon Peter Herbert	Lt Colonel	1988	31 Mar	9th/12th Royal Lancers
Liddell	Augustus Frederick	Captain	1895	27 Jul	Royal Artillery
Lindam	Charles James	Major	1854	May	Rifle Brigade
Lister, DSO	Frederick Hamilton	Lt Colonel	1932	13 Oct	Royal Artillery (DSO 1916)
Lithgow	William Samuel Plenderleath	Lt Colonel	1970	08 May	Royal Horse Artillery and 10th Royal Hussars
Little	James	Esq.	1846	Feb	
Lloyd	Joseph Skipp	Esq.	1843	Feb	

In The Room Of	Remarks
Holmes, William Henry (Resigned)	Resigned 1859
Bolton, Richard George (Captain) (Resigned)	Died 1865
Lewis, Hon Peter, (Lt Colonel) (Retired)	
Kenworthy, Edward Wilson (Resigned)	Died 1856
Previté, Kenneth E. OBE. (Lt Colonel)	Promoted Clerk of the Cheque 1981. Lieutenant 1986. CVO New Year 1990 Retired 1 Oct 1990
Smyth, Henry Sheppard (Resigned)	Died 1862
Hodgson, Peter. (Lt Colonel) (Retired)	
Talman, James John (Resigned)	Resigned 1845
Vandeleur, John O E. DSO* (Brigadier) (Resigned)	Died 31 July 1981
Hancock, Thomas	Resigned 1837
Lear, Charles (Resigned)	Resigned 1845
Norrie, Hon Guy, (Lt Colonel) Promoted Clerk of the Cheque	
Campbell, Charles F.CIE. (Lt Colonel) Promoted Clerk of the Cheque	Promoted Clerk of the Cheque 1935
Williams, Theodore, (Captain) (Half Pay)	Resigned 1932
Groves, Major Jeremy (Deceased)	
Salomons, Philip (Resigned)	Died 1854
Battye, Montagu John (Major) (Deceased)	Resigned 1928
Breitmeyer, Alan N. (Brigadier) Promoted Harbinger	Resigned 26 Mar 2008
Lister, Frederick. DSO. (Lt Colonel) (Retired 1950)	Retired 8 Mar 1977
Chamberlain, Sir Henry, Bt. (Resigned)	Resigned 1867
Woolley, John (Deceased)	Resigned 1844
Platt, George (Resigned)	Resigned 1854
Bulmer, Henry (Resigned)	Resigned 1837
Constable, George (Resigned)	Resigned 1856
Birkett, Frederick Blow (Resigned)	Died 1870
Daubeney, Frederick S (Captain) (Resigned)	Died 1870
Smiley, David de C, MVO, OBE, MC. (Colonel) Resigned	Retired 30 Mar 1988
Paget, Alwyn de B. (Colonel) (Deceased)	Retired 21 June 1953. (Kt Bach 1941. MVO 1953)
Breadalbane and Holland, The Earl of, MC. (Lt Colonel) (Resigned)	CO 5 DORSETS 1939.Resigned 1951. Deid 16 April 1955
Cox, Charles James (Resigned)	Died 1869
Fisher, John. OBE. (Lt Colonel) (Retired)	
Laurie, David A. St.G. OBE, MC. (Lt Colonel) (Retired)	Retired 2007
Edwards, Henry M. (Major) (Deceased)	Resigned 1926
Taylor, William Henry (Deceased)	Resigned 1877
Newton, J W Marsdin. (Brig General) (Deceased)	Retired 1950. Died 16 Nov 1971
St George, Frederick, F B. CVO. (Lt Colonel) (Deceased)	Retired 18 Feb 1990. Died 8 Aug 1997
Blenkarn, John (Resigned)	Resigned 1850
Nighingale, John (Resigned)	Promoted Clerk of the Cheque 1852

Surname	Christian Names	Rank	Year	Month	Regiment
Lloyd	William	Esq.	1850	Sep	
Lloyd	Wilford Neville	Major	1899	01 Jan	Royal Artillery
Lockhart	Brian Joseph	Lt Colonel	1987	11 May	Blues & Royals
Lonsdale	William	Esq.	1832	Mar	
Lowndes	James Fielder	Captain	1858	Nov	Renfrew Militia
Lowndes *(c)*	John Henry	Lt Colonel	1864	17 Dec	6th Foot
Lowther	Sir Charles Douglas, Bt. *(Son)*	Colonel	1997	18 May	Queen's Royal Irish Hussars
Lowther, OBE	Sir William Guy, Bt. *(Father)*	Lt Colonel	1962	06 Feb	8th King's Royal Irish Hussars
Lyon	William	Esq.	1844	May	
MacDougall	Stewart	Major	1900	11 May	Argyll & Sutherland Highlanders
Macfarlane	James Richard *(Brother)*	Lt Colonel	1990	18 Feb	Coldstream Guards
Macfarlane	Charles Keble *(Brother)*	Major	2006	24 Nov	Coldstream Guards
Macintosh	George Daniel	Esq.	1835	Nov	
MacKenzie-Beevor, CBE	Christopher David	Colonel	2002	24 Dec	1st The Queen's Dragoon Guards
MacNeil	Hector Archibald	Esq.	1833	Dec	
MacNeil	Hector Archibald	Esq.	1840	Jun	
MaCrae Gilstrap	John	Major	1901	05 Mar	Royal Highlanders (Black Watch)
Mahon	Sir William Walter, Bt.	Colonel	1993	10 Apr	Irish Guards
Mainwaring	Edwin George	Captain	1865	10 Mar	16th (Bedfordshire) Regiment of Foot
Maitland	Viscount Frederick Colin (Earl of Lauderdale)	Lt Colonel	1903	22 Dec	Scots Guards
Makgill Crichton Maitland, DSO	Mark Edward	Lt Colonel	1928	22 May	Grenadier Guards (DSO 4 Jan 1917)
Makins, DSO	Sir William Vivian, Bt.	Lt Colonel	1951	23 Nov	Welsh Guards
Malcolmson, VC, MVO *(m)*	John	Lieutenant	1870	25 May	3rd Bombay Light Cavalry
Maltravers	John	Esq.	1833	May	
Mansell Jones VC, CMG, DSO	Conwyn	Colonel	1920	10 Dec	West Yorkshire Regiment (DSO France 1915)
Markes	Alfred	Esq.	1841	Aug	
Marshall	William Julius	Esq.	1853	May	
Martin	Henry	Esq.	1825	Oct	
Matheson of Matheson	Sir Torquhil Alexander, Bt. *(Brother)*	Major	1977	16 Sep	Coldstream Guards
Matheson of Matheson	Fergus John (Sir Fergus John, Bt. from 1993) *(Brother)*	Major	1979	04 Feb	Coldstream Guards
Matthews	James	Esq.	1824	Jan	
Maud	John George	Esq.	1828	May	
Maxwell, OBE	Alexander Gordon	Lt Colonel	1919	18 Mar	11th (King Edward VII's Own) Lancers (Probyn's Horse)
Mayfield, DSO	Richard	Lt Colonel	1981	02 Nov	Scots Guards (DSO Northern Ireland)
McCall *(c)*	William	Lt Colonel	1860?	Unattached list	
McCallum	George Kellie	Lt Colonel	1889	28 May	Gordon Highlanders
McCoy	Thomas Robert	Captain	1852	May	65th (2nd Yorkshire, North Riding) Regiment of Foot

In The Room Of	Remarks
Hay, Robert Bryce (Resigned)	Resigned 1852
Cuninghame, William C (Captain) (Half Pay)	Promoted 1925
Speke, Neil H R. MC. (Major) (Retired)	Resigned 31 Jan 1996. Died 11 Feb 1996
Robe, John William (Resigned)	Resigned 1835
Neville, Percy (Promoted Lt Colonel) (P W) (Resigned)	Resigned 1870
Sawyer, Charles Richard J (Captain) (Resigned)	Half Pay 1903
Colenso Jones, Mervyn. (Major) Promoted Harbinger	
Digby, The Lord, KG, DSO, MC, TD (Colonel) (Resigned)	Died 7 May 1982
Vaughan, John (Resigned)	Resigned 1852
Clarke, John Walround (Captain) (Half Pay)	Killed in Action 1915
Lithgow, William S.P. (Lt Colonel) (Retired)	Retired 9 Apr 2009
ffrench Blake, Robert (Colonel) Promoted Harbinger	
Hoy, Isaac Alexander (Resigned)	Resigned 1843
Crossley, Hon Nicholas, OBE, TD (Colonel) (Retired)	
Nicholls, John Warner (Resigned)	Resigned 1836
Adamthwaite, John Allen (Resigned)	Resigned 1847
Rogers, John Edward V. (Lt Colonel) (Deceased)	Resigned 1936
Hall, Thomas, OBE. (Colonel) Promoted Clerk of the Cheque	Promoted Clerk of the Cheque 2006. Standard Bearer 2008
Robinson, Frederick John (Resigned)	Died 1869
Willan, S. L. Douglas (Captain) (Half Pay)	Died 1931
Keppel, Edward George (Colonel) (Resigned)	Retired CVO 1952. Died 30 Jan 1972
Paley, Alan T. CMG, DSO. (Colonel) (Retired 1946)	Died 1969
Secretan, D.G. (Resigned)	Resigned 1838
Mildmay, H A St John (Lt Colonel) (Resigned)	Died 1942
Charnock, Richard (Resigned)	Resigned 1848
Peters, James (Major) (Resigned)	Resigned 1856
Gibbons, Randall	Resigned 1838
Hamilton Russell, Hon R. DSO. (Brigadier) Promoted Standard Bearer	Promoted Clerk of the Cheque 1990. Died 9 Apr 1993
Crichton, Richard J V. MC. (Colonel) Promoted Clerk of the Cheque	Promoted Standard Bearer, 1993. Retired 22 Feb 1997
Smith, George	Resigned 1841
Harris, William	Resigned 1849
Berkeley, Thomas Mowbray (Lt Colonel) (Killed in action)	Died 1936
Eagles, C.E.James. (Lt Colonel) Promoted Harbinger	Promoted Clerk of the Cheque 14 Mar 1994. Lieutenant 1998
	Retired LVO, 2000. Died 30 Nov 2007
	Promoted Clerk of the Cheque 1863. Standard Bearer Sept 1872. Died 1875
Vance, Horatio Page (Lt Colonel) (Resigned)	Died 1899
Hay, Robert Bryce (Resigned)	Resigned 1858

Surname	Christian Names	Rank	Year	Month	Regiment
Mercer	James	Esq.	1837	Oct	
Messiter *(c)*	Sussex L A B	Captain	1864	25 Apr	28th (North Gloucestershire) regiment of Foot
Middleton	William Handcock	Esq.	1854	May	
Mildmay *(c)*	Herbert Alexander St.John	Lt Colonel	1885	16 Oct	Rifle Brigade
Mills	Francis Vanderlure	Esq.	1848	Nov	
Milner	Edward	Major	1905	06 May	Scots Guards
Mitford, CB, DSO	Bertram Reveley	Brig General	1912	29 Feb	East Surrey Regiment (DSO South Africa)
Mitford, CMG	William Kenyon	Lt Colonel	1900	01 Dec	8th Hussars
Mitford Slade	Cecil Townley	Colonel	1952	11 Jul	King's Royal Rifle Corps
Money *(m)*	George Noel, CB	Colonel	1885	09 Jan	Bengal Staff Corps
Monteagle of Brandon	Gerald Spring Rice, Baron.	Captain	1978	01 Apr	Irish Guards
Moore	Arthur Hinton	Esq.	1856	Jan	
Morrison *(c)*	John Charles Downie	Colonel	1869	02 Apr	Royal Marines
Mortimer	Thomas Bythesea	Lt Colonel	1861	22 Jul	Unattached List
Murray	Charles Edward	Esq.	1843	Dec	
Murray	Charles Wyndham	Colonel	1891	09 Jan	Seaforth Highlanders
Need *(m)*	Arthur	Lt Colonel	1867	06 May	14th (King's) Hussars
Nelson	John Raymond Ewing	Major	1988	22 Nov	Royal Green Jackets
Neville (P,W)	Percy	Major	1847	Mar	63rd (West Suffolk) Regiment of Foot
Newton	John Marsdin	Lt Colonel	1903	25 Apr	Royal Artillery
Nicholas	Griffin	Major	1861	17 Jul	5th (Northumberland Fusiliers) Rregiment of Foot
Nicholls	John Warner	Esq.	1831	Dec	
Nightingale	John	Esq.	1839	Dec	
Noel	Edward Andrew	Captain	1875	19 Mar	31st (Huntingdonshire) Regiment of Foot
Norrie	Hon Guy Bainbridge	Lt Colonel	1990	31 Jul	Royal Hussars (PWO)
Nunn	Joshua Anthony James	Major	1979	04 May	10th Hussars
Ogilvie	John Gilbert	Captain	1845	Mar	92nd Highlanders (Gordon)
O'Kelly	Augustus de Pentheny	Esq.	1848	Oct	
Oldham	Henry Hugh	Colonel	1887	12 Feb	Cameron Highlanders
Orme	Frederick Doveton	Esq.	1833	Sep	
Owen	Arthur Allen	Colonel	1885	03 Mar	88th (Connaught Rangers) Regiment of Foot
Paget	Alwyn de Blacquiere	Colonel	1903	23 Nov	Durham Light Infantry
Paley, CMG, DSO	Alan Thomas	Colonel	1925	02 Feb	Rifle Brigade (DSO France 1915
Palliser	Arthur	Esq.	1858	Apr	
Pardoe	Philip	Colonel	1970	02 Jan	Royal Green Jackets
Pavy *(m)*	Francis	Captain	1869	20 Jul	74th Highlanders (Later Highland Light Infantry)
Peake, DSO, OBE	Roger	Brigadier	1953	23 Jun	Royal Dragoons
Pepys, DSO	Anthony Hilton	Brigadier	1951	03 Aug	Royal Dragoons

In The Room Of	Remarks
Hemsley, Henry (Resigned)	Resigned 1838
Dampier, Stephen Ryder (Captain) (Resigned)	Died 1870
Cotter, Sir James Laurence, Bt. (Resigned)	Resigned 1870
Goodwin, Edward (Major) (Resigned)	Resigned 1920. Chairman Army & Navy Club 1880-81, 1886-87, 1904-05
Walker, Thomas Richard (Resigned)	Resigned 1865
Clement, Reynold A (Lt Colonel) (Resigned)	Resigned 1933
Scott, William Angel (Lt Colonel) Promoted Harbinger. Sub Officer 1927	Died 1936
Fletcher, Henry A (Colonel) Promoted Clerk of the Cheque	Retired 1938 (CVO 1937)
Buckley, Basil T.CB, CMG, CVO. (Brig General) Promoted Standard Bearer 1946	Retired 19 Apr 1973. Died 13 Aug 1986
Sutherland, Edward (Major) (Deceased)	Died 1895
Sinclair, Thomas C. OBE, MC. (Lt Colonel) (Resigned)	Retired 5 Jul 1996
Pope, William Agnew (Resigned)	Resigned 1861
Boggis Rolfe, James E (Captain) (Resigned)	Half Pay 1895
Rich, Sir Charles, Bt.	Half Pay 1881
Hopkinson, Francis (Resigned)	Resigned 1845
Dunbar,William M (Lt Colonel) (Half Pay)	Resigned 1912
Killery, James (Resigned)	Appt Exon, Yeomen of the Guard 1869. Lieut Yeomen 1876
Dillon, J Desmond, DSC. (Major) (Deceased)	Resigned (moving overseas) 11 Sep 1993
Ogilvie, John Gilbert, (Resigned)	Resigned 1858
Wemyss, Francis C. (Colonel) (Resigned) The last Gentleman to resign who had purchased his place.	Died 1932
Moore, Arthur Hinton (Resigned)	Half Pay 1883
Wright, Charles (Resigned)	Resigned 1833
Wood, Samuel (Resigned)	Resigned 1843
Toogood, Alexander D. (Captain) (Deceased)	Died 1899
Suffield, The Lord, MC. (Major) Promoted Harbinger	Promoted Clerk of the Cheque 2003. Lieutenant 2006
Perry, Robert S, DSO. (Lt Colonel) (Retired)	Retired 26 Mar 1997.
Johnston, Thomas Hayter (Resigned)	Resigned 1847
Vardon, Erin (Resigned)	Resigned 1851
Granville, Bevill (Major) (Half Pay)	Promoted 1887 Clerk of the Cheque (Year of joining). Lieutenant 1891. Retired 1922
Dutton, William (Resigned)	Resigned 1835
Ellison, Richard George (Major) (Resigned)	Died 1917
Brown, Edward (Colonel) (Half Pay)	Died 1931
LLoyd, Wilford N. CB. Promoted Clerk of the Cheque	Retired 1946. Died 1950.
McCoy, Thomas Robert (Resigned)	Resigned 1877
Granville, John (Lt Colonel) (Resigned)	Promoted Harbinger 1986. Drowned 1987
Mainwaring, Edwin (Captain) (Deceased)	Half Pay 1882
Vesey, Hon Osbert E. CBE. (Lt Colonel) Promoted Clerk of the Cheque 1948. Standard Bearer 1953, Lieutenant 1955 (Resigned 1956)	Died 1959
Dillon Eric F, Viscount CMG, DSO (Colonel) (Retired 1946)	Died 1967

Surname	Christian Names	Rank	Year	Month	Regiment
Perkins	Alfred	Esq.	1839	Feb	
Perry, DSO	Robert Stanley	Lt Colonel	1959	12 Jun	9th Queen's Royal Lancers
Peters	James	Major	1853	Apr	Regiment not recorded
Peters	James	Major	1859	Aug	Not known
Peto	James Fielder	Esq.	1850	Nov	
Peto	William Gurth	Major	2000	02 Nov	13th/18th Royal Hussars (QMO)
Philips	Nathaniel George	Captain	1858	Jul	47th (Lancashire) Regiment of Foot
Platt	George	Esq.	1838	Mar	
Pocklington *(c) (m)*	George Henry	Lt Colonel	1877	01 Jul	18th (Royal Irish) Regiment of Foot
Pollen, CMG	Stephen Hungerford	Lt Colonel	1919	18 Mar	Wiltshire Regiment
Pope	William Agnew	Esq.	1855	Mar	
Potter, OBE	Cyril Charles Hamilton	Captain	1919	18 Mar	10th Hussars
Previté, OBE	Kenneth Edward	Lt Colonel	1945	18 Sep	Royal Marines
Price	Francis Lysons	Esq.	1839	Apr	
Price Davies, VC, CB, CMG, DSO	Llewelyn Alberic Emilius	Major General	1933	13 Jul	King's Royal Rifle Corps (DSO South Africa 1901)
Pryce Jones, DSO, MVO, MC	Henry Morris	Colonel	1922	15 Dec	Coldstream Guards
Purdon, OBE	Timothy Corran Richard	Colonel	2000	04 Sep	Irish Guards and Welsh Guards
Pyrke	Duncombe	Esq.	1853	Mar	
Ramsden	Edward	Esq.	1828	Feb	
Ramsden, MBE	Ivor Basil	Major	1979	20 Jul	Welsh Guards
Rasch	Sir Frederick Carne, Bt.	Colonel	1929	09 Jul	6th Dragoon Guards
Rasch	Sir Richard Guy Carne, Bt.	Major	1968	23 Jul	Grenadier Guards
Raymond	George	Esq.	1842	Apr	
Reeve	Thomas Newby	Esq.	1827	Jan	
Reid, OBE	Percy Fergus Ivo	Colonel	1961	03 Nov	Irish Guards
Ricardo	Henry William Ralph	Major	1903	13 Apr	17th Lancers
Rice	Herbert Henry	Esq.	1848	Nov	
Rice	George Watkin	Major	1853	Oct	23rd (Royal Welch Fusiliers) Regiment of Foot
Rich	Sir Charles Henry John,	Bt.	1859	Mar	
Richbell	Thomas	Esq.	1845	Feb	
Roach	Richard Gater	Esq.	1851	Aug	
Robe	John William	Esq.	1828	Oct	
Robe	John William	Esq.	1833	Feb	
Robertson	Henry	Esq.	1853	Dec	
Robertson	Charles Alexander Lockhart	Dr.	1856	May	Staff Asst Surgeon.
Robertson, MC	Michael John Calverley	Colonel	1994	14 Mar	Royal Green Jackets (MC Borneo)
Robinson	William	Esq.	1841	Feb	
Robinson	John James	Esq.	1844	Feb	
Robinson	Frederick John	Esq.	1856	Apr	
Rodwell	John Francis Meadows	Major	1998	13 Apr	Grenadier Guards

In The Room Of	Remarks
Blackmore, Robert (Resigned)	Resigned 1848
Daly, Victor A H. OBE, MC. (Brevet Lt Colonel) (Resigned 1951)	Retired 4 May 1979. Died 11 Apr 1987
Topham, William. Promoted Lieutenant and knighted	Resigned 1853
Field, Aesculapius (Resigned)	Resigned 1863
Gordon, John (Resigned)	Resigned 1859
Cockcroft, Barnaby (Major) Promoted Clerk of the Cheque	
Hopton, Charles Edward (Resigned)	Resigned 1874
Maltravers, John (Resigned)	Resigned 1846
Gifford, John Wynter (Captain) (Deceased)	Half Pay 1905. Chairman Army & Navy Club 1892-93, 1894-95, 1896-97
Campbell, Hon Ivan (Captain) (Died on active service 1917)	Resigned 1935
Pyrke, Duncombe (Resigned)	Resigned 1856
Owen, Arthur Allen MVO (Colonel) (Deceased)	Resigned 1932
Mansel Jones, Conwyn, VC, CMG, DSO (Colonel) (Deceased 1942)	Retired 12 Sep 1968. Died 9 May 1971
Robe, John William (Resigned)	Resigned 1844
Milner, Edward (Major) (Resigned)	Retired 30 June 1948. Died 1965
Davidson, Christopher M (Colonel) (Deceased)	Promoted Harbinger 1938. Standard Bearer 1949. Resigned CVO June 1952. Died 5 Nov 1952
Baker, James, MBE. (Colonel) Promoted Harbinger	
Robinson, John James (Resigned)	Resigned 1854
Tucker, William	Resigned 1833
Reid, PF Ivo, OBE (Colonel) Promoted Harbinger	Retired 1999
Forbes Leith, (Burn), Charles (Colonel) (Resigned)	Resigned 1938
Fulford, Francis E.A. (Lt Colonel) (Retired)	Retired 10 Oct 1988. Died 24 Jun 1996
Sams, William (Resigned)	Resigned 1842
Griffiths, Thomas	Promoted 1836 Appointment not clear
Ormonde, Marquess of. MC. (Lt Colonel) Promoted Clerk of the Cheque	Promoted Harbinger 1979. Retired 2 Nov 1981. Died 9 Dec 1994
Lowndes, John Henry (Colonel) (Resigned)	Retired 1938 (CVO 1939)
Richbell, Thomas (Resigned)	Resigned 1853
Rice, Henry Herbert (Resigned)	Resigned 1856
Hayward, Edward (Resigned)	Resigned 1861
Gregory, John (Resigned)	Resigned 1848
de Blaquiere, Robert Milley (Resigned)	Resigned 1853
Holbrook, Joseph	Resigned 1832
Gibson, Robert (Resigned)	Resigned 1839
Shield, Peter Ralph (Resigned)	Resigned 1856
Grange, Robert (Captain) (Resigned)	Resigned 1858
Mayfield, Richard, DSO. (Lt Colonel) Promoted Clerk of the Cheque	
Gray, Thomas (Resigned)	Resigned 1843
Walker, Matthew Clement (Resigned)	Resigned 1853
Cargill, William Walter. Promoted Clerk of the Cheque	Resigned 1865
Fanshawe, David, OBE (Colonel) Promoted Clerk of the Cheque	

Surname	Christian Names	Rank	Year	Month	Regiment
Rowley	Hon William Chambre	Major	1899	01 Jan	Royal Artillery
Russell	Jeremy Andrew Newton	Major	2009	09 Apr	Royal Green Jackets
Russell, CVO, CBE, DSO	Reginald Edmund Maghlin	Colonel	1931	13 Nov	Royal Engineers (DSO 1915, Suez Canal Operations)
Salomons	Philip	Esq.	1848	Dec	
Salomons	Philip	Esq.	1854	Mar	REJOIN
Sams	William	Esq.	1832	Jan	
Sandeman (c)	James Glas	Captain	1869	22 Jun	1st (Royal) Dragoons
Saunders	Henry Frederick	Lt Colonel	1861	18 Jul	West India Regiment
Savill, DSO	Kenneth Edward	Colonel	1955	29 Mar	Queen's Bays
Sawyer	Charles Richard John	Captain	1856	May	2nd Somerset Militia
Schofield VC	Henry Norton	Major	1911	03 May	Royal Artillery
Scott	William Angel	Lt Colonel	1901	01 Jul	Cameron Highlanders
Scott	Sir James Walter, Bt.	Lt Colonel	1977	08 Mar	Grenadier Guards and Life Guards
Scott (c) (m)	Francis Cunningham, CB	Colonel	1878	28 Dec	42nd (Royal Highland) Regiment of Foot Black Watch
Scott, CMG, DSO	Lord Herbert Montagu Douglas	Lt Colonel	1922	02 Jun	Irish Guards (DSO South Africa)
Secretan	D.G.	Esq.	1829	Sep	
Shakeshaft	Charles	Esq.	1838	Aug	
Shield	Peter Ralph	Esq.	1845	May	
Simmons	Thomas Charles	Esq.	1835	Apr	
Sinclair, OBE, MC	Thomas Christopher	Lt Colonel	1965	24 Sep	Rifle Brigade
Skeffington Smyth, DSO	Geoffrey Henry Julian	Lt Colonel	1920	07 May	9th Lancers
Smiley, MVO,OBE,MC	David de Crespigny	Colonel	1966	28 Jan	Royal Horse Guards
Smith	Henry Webb	Esq.	1831	Apr	
Smith	James Norton	Esq.	1840	Mar	
Smith, DSO	Herbert Frederick Edgar	Lt Colonel	1936	21 Jul	King's Royal Rifle Corps (DSO Great War)
Smyth	Henry Sheppard	Esq.	1850	Aug	
Somerset	Lord Henry Edward Brudenall	Lieutenant	1884	19 Feb	Royal Horse Guards
Speke, MC	Neil Hanning Reid	Lt Colonel	1967	20 Mar	12th Royal Lancers
Spragge, DSO	Basil Edward	Major	1900	19 Mar	King's Own Yorkshire Light Infantry (DSO Burma 1887)
St George, CVO	Frederick Ferris Bligh	Lt Colonel	1957	11 Sep	Life Guards
St. Aubyn	Thomas Edward	Major	1973	07 May	King's Royal Rifle Corps
Stapleton Cotton	Charles	Esq.	1849	Oct	
Steele	William	Esq.	1840	Jun	
Steele, MBE	Robert	Lt Colonel	1969	03 Jun	Grenadier Guards
Stewart	James Ainslie	Colonel	1869	04 Jun	Royal Marines
Stewart	Rupert	Lt Colonel	1919	18 Mar	Duke of Cornwall's Light Infantry
Suffield, MC	Anthony Philip, Baron	Major	1973	20 Apr	Coldstream Guards
Sutherland	Edward	Major	1852	Feb	7th Foot, (Royal Fusiliers)

In The Room Of	Remarks
McCallum, George K (Lt Colonel) (Deceased)	Resigned 1922
MacFarlane, Richard (Lt Colonel) (Retired)	
Schofield, Harry. VC (Lt Colonel) (Deceased)	Military Attaché Buenos Aires 1939. Retired 1949. Died 1950.
Perkins, Alfred (Resigned)	Resigned 1852
Kitson, George (Resigned)	Resigned 1858
Geary, William (Resigned)	Resigned 1842
Need, Arthur (Lt Colonel) (Resigned)	Promoted 1874 (Historian)
Bentley, Frederick Stocks (Resigned)	Resigned 1868
Wingfield, Hon Maurice. CMG, CVO, DSO (Maj General) Promoted Standard Bearer 1952	Promoted Standard Bearer 1972. Lieutenant 1973. Retired CVO 8 Aug 1976
Davies, Richard Edward (Resigned)	Resigned 1864
Cooch, Charles (Colonel) Resigned)	Died 1931
Stewart, James Ainslie (Colonel) (Deceased)	Promoted Harbinger 1912
Kidston Montgomerie, George, DSO, MC, (Colonel) (Retired)	Promoted Standard Bearer 1990. Lieutenant 13 Jun 1993. Died 2 Nov 1993 after a hunting accident
Tilbrook, Philip L. (Major) (Promoted)	Resigned 1888
Dick Cunynghame, Sir W, Bt., CBE (Major) (Deceased)	Resigned 1935
Page, Samuel (Resigned)	Resigned 1833
Mercer, James (Resigned)	Died 1843
Ellis, Francis (Resigned)	Resigned 1853
Bullock, Daniel (Resigned)	Resigned 1840
Colvin, John F. OBE,MC. (Lt Colonel) (Retired 24 Sep 1965)	Resigned 1 April 1978
Gore, St.John C, (Colonel) Promoted	Died 1939
Cheney, John N. OBE. (Brigadier) Promoted Standard Bearer	Resigned 1968
Dowling, Maurice (Resigned)	Resigned 1840
Smith, Henry Webb (Resigned)	Resigned 1844
MacRae Gilstrap, John (Lt Colonel) (Resigned)	Died on Active Service 1940
Blake, Theobald (Resigned)	Resigned 1861
Hardinge, Henry (Lt Colonel) (Resigned)	Resigned 1896
Pepys, Anthony H, DSO (Brigadier) (Deceased)	Retired 11 May 1987. Died 22 Oct 1996.
Wallack, Henry T (Captain) (Half Pay)	Died 1926
Edwards Guy Janion DSO, MC (Colonel) (Retired 1951)	Died 4 April 1970
Clifton, Peter T, DSO. (Colonel) Promoted Clerk of the Cheque (Retired 13 Jun 1993)	Promoted Clerk of the Cheque 1986. Lieutenant 1990. CVO New Year 1993
Denne, George (Resigned)	Resigned 1902
Simmons, Thomas Charles (Resigned)	Resigned 1848
Makins, Sir William V, Bt., DSO (Lt Colonel) (Deceased)	Promoted Harbinger 1987. Retired 31 Jul 1990. Died 21 Nov 1995
Leith, James VC (Major) (Deceased)	Died 1901
MacDougall, Stewart (Lt Colonel) (Killed in action)	Died 1930
Mitford Slade, Cecil T. (Colonel) (Retired)	Promoted Harbinger 1990. Retired 1992
Smith, Sir Benjamin (Deceased)	Died 1884

Surname	Christian Names	Rank	Year	Month	Regiment	
Swetenham, DSO	John Edmund	Brigadier	1959	16 Apr	Royal Scots Greys	
Talman	James John	Esq.	1834	Aug		
Talman	Francis Henry	Esq.	1836	May		
Taylor	William Henry	Captain	1850	Oct	87th (Royal Irish Fusiliers) Regiment of Foot	
Taylor *(c)*	William O'Bryen	Major	1867	06 May	22nd (The Cheshire) Regiment of Foot	
Templemore, Baron	Dermot Richard Claud, later Marquess of Donegall	Major	1966	07 Feb	7th Queen's Own Hussars	
Thomson	James	Esq.	1838	Feb		
Thynne, CMG, DSO	Ulric Oliver	Colonel	1922	02 Jun	King's Royal Rifle Corps (DSO Wiltshire Yeomanry South Africa)	
Tillbrook *(c)*	Philip Limborch	Major	1873	23 Dec	Unattached List	
Tinkler	William Alexander	Esq.	1848	Jun		
Tomkins	Benjamin	Esq.	1835	Feb		
Toogood *(c) (m)*	Alexander Decimus	Captain	1862	11 Aug	104th Foot (2nd Royal Munster Fusiliers)	
Topham	William	Esq.	1850	Mar		
Towse VC	Ernest Beechcroft Beckwith	Captain	1903	01 Jan	Gordon Highlanders	
Traherne	Rhodri Llewellyn	Lt Colonel	2008	26 Mar	Welsh Guards	
Trick	Frederick John	Esq.	1842	Jul		
Tufnell	Edward	Lt Colonel	1894	30 Mar	Royal Irish Rifles	
Tyler	John	Esq.	1824	Dec		
Tyler	James	Esq.	1843	Jan		
Tyler	Charles	Captain	1850	Jan		
Vance *(c)*	Horatio Page	Lt Colonel	1874	27 Feb	38th (1st Staffordshire) Regiment of Foot	
Vandeleur, DSO*	John Ormsby Evelyn	Brigadier	1953	23 Jun	Irish Guards	
Vardon	Erin	Esq.	1846	Feb		
Varty Rogers *(m)*	John Edward	Lt Colonel	1887	27 Apr	102nd Foot, 1st Royal Dublin Fusiliers.	
Vaughan	John	Esq.	1833	Aug		
Vesey, CBE (CMG 1950)	Hon Osbert Eustace	Lt Colonel	1922	02 Jun	9th Lancers	
Villiers	Charles Hyde	Major	1907	15 May	Royal Horse Guards	
Vivian, CMG, DSO, MVO	Valentine	Lt Colonel	1926	09 Mar	Grenadier Guards	
Vyvyan	Richard Henry Stackhouse	Lieutenant	1859	Jul	Cornwall Rangers	
Walker	Matthew Clement	Esq.	1833	Aug		
Walker	John Tyrwhitt	Esq.	1841	Jan		
Walker	Thomas Richard	Esq.	1845	Jun		
Walker	William	Esq.	1857	Aug		
Walker (Campbell Walker) *(m)*	Arthur Campbell	Captain	1869	20 Jul	79th Regiment of Foot, or Queen's Own Cameron Highlanders	
Wallack	Henry Jobling	Captain	1864	17 Dec	77th (East Middlesex) Regiment of Foot	
Waller *(m)*	John Hampden	Lieutenant	1870	26 Aug	28th Foot	
Walsh	Frederick	Esq.	1828	Mar		
Walsh	Thomas George	Esq.	1837	Apr		

In The Room Of	Remarks
Cuninghame, William W S. DSO. (Lt Colonel) (Retired 1959)	Retired 1 May 1979. Died Kenya 13 Feb 1982
Walsh, Frederick (Resigned)	Resigned 1840
Reeve, Thomas Newby. Promoted (Appointment not clear)	Resigned 1844
Green, David (Resigned)	Died 1854
Hanning, James (Resigned)	Promoted Clerk of the Cheque 1872. Standard Bearer 1876
Chandos Pole, John, OBE. (Lt Colonel) Promoted Harbinger	Promoted Standard Bearer, 9 Jan 1984. Retired LVO 18 Apr 1986
Belcher, John Moulden (Resigned)	Resigned 1850
Gore, Charles C (Colonel) (Resigned)	Promoted Standard Bearer 1945. (CVO,TD)
Hume, Henry CB, (Colonel) (Resigned)	Promoted Clerk of the Cheque 1878. Standard Bearer 1886
Markes, Alfred (Resigned)	Resigned 1854
Howse, George (Resigned)	Resigned 1849
Cockney, James Wentworth (Resigned)	Died 1874
Little, James (Resigned)	Promoted Lieutenant 1853.Resigned 1859
Bourke, Paget John. (Captain) (Half Pay)	Retired 1939 (KCVO,CBE). Died 21 June 1948. MBE 1919
Ker, Roger. MC (Lt Colonel) (Resigned)	
Raymond, George (Resigned)	Resigned 1846
Hennell, Reginald (Lt Colonel) DSO (Resigned - to Yeomen)	Died 1909
Grinly, William (No details of departure)	Died 1833
Macintosh, George Daniel (Resigned)	Resigned 1850
Tyler, James, (Resigned)	Resigned 1875
Philips, Nathaniel G. (Captain) (Resigned)	Appt Exon, Yeomen of the Guard 1889
Price Davies, L A E. VC , CB, CMG, DSO. (Major Gen) (Retired 1948)	Resigned 1 June 1973
Hodgson, Henry Sibley (Resigned)	Resigned 1848
Walker, Arthur Campbell (Captain) (Deceased)	Died 1901
Caulfield, Daniel (Resigned)	Resigned 1844
Carleton, Frederick M, DSO (Brig General) (Deceased)	Promoted Clerk of the Cheque 1948. Standard Bearer 1953. Lieutenant 1955 Resigned KCVO 12 Oct 1956
Brackenbury, Henry (Major) (Deceased)	Resigned 1939. (Lt Colonel CVO). Died 1947.
Spragge, Basil E, DSO. (Lt Colonel) (Deceased)	(First Head of MI6 Counter Espionage Unit. Died 1948 while Clerk of the Cheque & Adjutant)
Walker, William (Resigned)	Resigned 1864
Ramsden, Edward (Resigned)	Resigned 1844
Wilkinson, James (Resigned)	Resigned 1848
Carver, Edward Furst (Resigned)	Resigned 1848
Champion, Thomas Lyford (Resigned)	Resigned 1859
Doncaster, Harwick (Captain) (Resigned)	Died 1887
Barnard, Markland (Resigned)	Half Pay 1898
Lowndes, James (Major) (Resigned)	Resigned 1931
Wilkinson, Matthew (No details of departure)	Resigned 1834
Blackmore, Robert (Resigned)	Resigned 1842

Surname	Christian Names	Rank	Year	Month	Regiment
Walsh, DSO, OBE, MC	Robert Henry	Colonel	1938	18 Nov	Royal Artillery (DSO and MC Great War)
Warren	Jeremy Frederick	Major	1996	31 Jan	Scots Guards
Watts	Francis	Esq.	1842	Jun	
Way, MC	Anthony Gerald	Colonel	1972	07 Mar	Grenadier Guards
Webber	Raymond Sudeley	Major	1914	02 May	Royal Welch Fusiliers
Webster	Richard Michael Otley	Major	1993	16 Nov	Royal Horse Artillery
Weir	Hector Francis	Esq.	1830	Oct	
Wemyss	Francis Charteris	Lt Colonel	1860	Nov	Royal Wiltshire Militia
Wheatley	Francis	Lt Colonel	1856	Jun	
Wheatley, CMG, DSO	Leonard Lane	Brig General	1926	13 May	Argyll & Sutherland Highlanders (DSO 1898, North West Frontie
White	Henry Paget	Captain	1854	May	Madras Army
Whittington, MBE	Rev Richard Hugh	Colonel	1999	24 May	Royal Engineers
Wigram, MVO	Hon Andrew Francis Clive	Major	2000	14 Sep	Grenadier Guards
Willan (c)	Stanhope Leonard Douglas	Captain	1863	07 Oct	2nd or Queen's Royal Regiment of Foot
Williams	Benjamin Rennington	Captain	1856	Jun	Bengal Horse Artillery
Williams (c)	Theodore	Lieutenant	1871	05 Mar	10th The Prince of Wales's Own Royal Hussars
Wilson	Timothy John Michael	Colonel	1984	09 Jan	Royal Marines
Winchester	George	Esq.	1838	Jan	
Wingfield, CMG, DSO	Hon Maurice Anthony	Colonel	1928	28 Apr	Rifle Brigade
Winter	Charles	Esq.	1843	Jan	
Wise	William	Esq.	1860	May	
Woolley	John	Esq.	1830	Mar	
Worgan, CSI, CVO, DSO	Rivers Berney	Brig General	1932	07 Mar	Indian Army (DSO 1917)
Wright	Charles	Esq.	1825	Mar	
Wright	Thomas George	Esq.	1832	Jan	
Wright, VC, CB, CMG, DSO	Wallace Duffield	Brig General	1932	13 Oct	Royal West Surrey Regiment (The Queen's) (DSO 1918)
Wyatt (m)	Charles Edwyn	Brevet Major	1869	20 Jul	5th (Royal Irish) Lancers

In The Room Of	Remarks
Rasch, Sir Carne, Bt. ADC. (Colonel) (Resigned)	Retired 1954
Lockhart, Brian J. (Lt Colonel) (Resigned)	
Dance, Charles (Resigned)	Resigned 1854
Savill, Kenneth E, DSO. (Colonel) Promoted Standard Bearer	Promoted Standard Bearer 1988. Retired 5 Nov 1990
Hill, Augustus James (Lt Colonel) (Resigned)	Resigned 1935
Duncombe, Sir Philip, Bt. (Major) Promoted Harbinger	
King, Thomas (Resigned)	Resigned 1837
Wheatley, Francis (Lt Colonel) (Resigned)	Resigned 1903. Last serving Gentleman to purchase his place
White, Henry Paget (Major) (Resigned)	Resigned 1860
Liddell, Augustus F. CVO. (Captain) (Resigned)	Retired 1946. Died 7 June 1954
MacDonald, Gregory Grant (Resigned)	Resigned 1856
Arkwright, Anthony. (Major) Promoted Standard Bearer	Chaplain, The Royal Hospital Chelsea
Fox, Simon, OBE. (Colonel) (Resigned)	
Gridley, Henry Gillet (Resigned)	Half Pay 1903
Grange, Richard George (Captain) (Resigned)	Resigned 1859
Howard, Thomas. (Resigned)	Half Pay 1889
Donegall, Dermot Marquess of. Promoted Standard Bearer	Retired 2002
Martin, Henry (Resigned)	Resigned 1866
Gore Browne, Harold (Colonel) (Resigned)	Promoted Harbinger 1946. Retired 21 Jun 1953
Robinson, William (Resigned)	Resigned 1846
Domville, William. (Captain) (Resigned)	Resigned 1861
Vernon, Levison (Resigned)	Resigned 1839
Kelsey, Walter F (Colonel) (Resigned)	Died 1934
Spencer, John	Resigned 1831
Pearn, Robert (Resigned)	Resigned 1852
Potter, Cyril C H. OBE (Major) (Resigned)	Retired 1945. Died 1953. Chairman Army & Navy Club 1943-45
Cotton, George Finch (Resigned)	Half Pay 1895

Captains

A bracketed number indicates more than one tour as Captain

Date	Name
	HENRY VIII 1509-1547
1509	Henry Bourchier, Earl of Essex, KG
1526	Sir Anthony Browne, KG
1541	William Parr, Earl of Essex, KG, later Marquis of Northampton
	EDWARD VI 1547-1553
	William Parr, KG, Marquis of Northampton
	MARY 1553-1558
	Thomas Ratcliffe, Earl of Sussex, KG
	ELIZABETH I, 1558-1603
	Thomas Ratcliffe, Earl of Sussex, KG
1583	Henry Carey, Baron Hunsdon, KG
1596	George Carey, Baron Hunsdon, KG
	JAMES I 1605-1625
	George Carey, Baron Hunsdon, KG (Deceased)
1603	Henry Percy Earl of Northumberland, KG,
	(Convicted of Misprision of Treason 1606)
1606	Thomas Howard, Earl of Suffolk, KG
1614	Theophilus Howard, Lord Howard of Walden
	CHARLES I, 1625-1649
	Theophilus Howard, Lord Howard of Walden (Earl of Suffolk,
	and KG 1626)
1635	William Earl of Salisbury, KG
1643	Thomas, Earl of Cleveland (1)
1644	Francis, Lord Dunsmore (later Earl of Chester).
	THE COMMONWEALTH, 1649-1660
	CHARLES II, 1660-1685
1660	Thomas, Earl of Cleveland (2)
1667	John, Lord Bellasyse of Worlaby
1673	Thomas Bellasyse, Viscount Fauconberg
1674	Wentworth Dillon, Earl of Roscommon
1677	Robert, Lord Deincourt (Earl of Scarsdale 1680)
1683	Theophilus, Earl of Huntingdon
	JAMES II, 1685-1689
	Theophilus, Earl of Huntingdon
	WILLIAM & MARY, 1689-1702
1689	John, Lord Lovelace (Died 1693)
1693	Charles, Duke of St Albans, KG (1) (Natural son of Charles II)
	ANNE, 1702-1714
	Charles, Duke of St Albans, KG

Date	Name
1712	Henry Somerset, Duke of Beaufort, KG. (Died 1714)
	GEORGE I, 1714-1727
1714	Charles, Duke of St Albans, KG (2)
1726	William, Marquis of Hartington
	GEORGE II, 1727-1760
	William, Marquis of Hartington (Duke of Devonshire 1729)
1731	Richard Boyle, Earl of Burlington and Cork, KG
1733	John, Lord Monson
1734	John, Duke of Montagu, KG, KB
1740	Charles Duke of Bolton, KG
1742	Allen, Lord Bathurst
1744	John, Lord Hobart, KB (Earl of Buckinghamshire 1746)
1756	John, Lord Berkeley of Stratton
	GEORGE III, 1760-1820
	John, Lord Berkeley of Stratton
1762	George Henry, Earl of Lichfield
1772	George Edgcombe (Rear Admiral)
1782	George, Lord de Ferrars (1)
1783, May 14)	George Bussey, Lord Villiers (Later Earl of Jersey)
1783, Dec 31	George, Lord de Ferrars (Earl of Leicester, 1784) (2)
1790	George Evelyn, Viscount Falmouth
1806	St Andrew, Lord StJohn of Bletsoe
1808	Richard, Earl of Mount Edgecumbe
1812	James George Stopford, Earl of Courtown
	GEORGE IV, 1820-1830
	James George Stopford, Earl of Courtown
1827	Henry Fleming Lee, Viscount Hereford (1)
	WILLIAM IV, 1830-1837
	Henry Fleming Lee, Viscount Hereford
1830	Thomas, 3rd Baron Foley
1833 May	Thomas Henry, 4th Baron Foley (Also Lieutenant May 1833)
1834, Dec 30)	Henry Fleming Lee, Viscount Hereford (2)
1835, May 6	Thomas Henry, Lord Foley (2)
	VICTORIA, 1837-1901
	Thomas Henry, Lord Foley
1841	John George Weld, 2nd Baron Forester
1846	Thomas Henry, Lord Foley (3)
1852	John William Montagu, 7th Earl of Sandwich
1852, Dec 30	Thomas Henry, Lord Foley (4)

Date	Name
1858	Henry John Chetwynd-Talbot, Lord Shrewsbury (Rear Admiral) (Earl of Shrewsbury and Talbot)
1859	Thomas Henry, Lord Foley (5)
1866	Charles Augustus Bennet, 6th Earl of Tankerville
1867	William Alleyne Cecil, 3rd Marquis of Exeter (1)
1868, Dec 12	Thomas Henry, Lord Foley (6)
1869, Dec 17	George Augustus Constantine Phipps, 2nd Marquis of Normanby
1871	Francis Thomas de Grey, 7th Earl of Cowper, KG
1874, Jan 1	Henry Edward Fox-Strangeway, Earl of Ilchester
1874, Mar 2	William Alleyne Cecil, 3rd Marquis of Exeter (2)
1875	Charles Jonathan Chetwynd Talbot, 19th Earl of Shrewsbury & Talbot
1877	George William, 9th Earl of Coventry (1)
1880	Alexander William George Duff, 6th Earl of Fife
1881, Jan 21	Charles Gordon, 11th Marquis of Huntly
1881, Jun 28	Charles Robert Wynn Carrington, 3rd Baron Carrington
1885, Jul 6	George William, 9th Earl of Coventry (2)
1886, Feb 10	Charles Douglas Richard Hanbury-Tracey, 4th Baron Sudeley
1886, Aug 5	George William, 7th Viscount Barrington (Deceased)
1886, Nov 24	Francis Robert, Earl of Rosslyn
1890	Charles Alfred Worsley Anderson-Pelham, 4th Earl of Yarborough
1892	George William Henry Venables, 7th Baron Vernon
1894	Edwin Francis Scudamore-Stanhope, 10th Earl of Chesterfield
1895	Henry Shutt, 2nd Baron Belper
	EDWARD VII, 1901-1910
	Henry Shutt, 2nd Baron Belper
1906	William Lygon ,7th Earl Beauchamp, KG, KCMG, PC
1907	Thomas, 3rd Baron Lord Denman (The Royal Scots)
	GEORGE V, 1910-1936
	Thomas, 3rd Baron Lord Denman (The Royal Scots) GCMG, GCVO
1911	Edward Arthur, 1st Baron Colebrook, PC, GCVO
1922	George Herbert Hyde Villiers, 6th Earl of Clarendon KG, PC, GCMG, GCVO, DL, JP(1)
1924, Feb 15	Major Alexander Edward Murray, Earl of Dunmore, VC, DSO, MVO
1924, Dec 5	George Herbert Hyde Villiers, 6th Earl of Clarendon, KG, PC, GCMG, GCVO, DL, JP(2) (Died 1955)
1925	Ivor Miles Windsor-Clive, 2nd Earl of Plymouth (Worcestershire Yeomanry)
1929, Jan 1	Brig General Sir George Charles Bingham, 5th Earl of Lucan, KBE, CB, TD (Rifle Brigade) (1)
1929, Jul 1	General Frederick Rudolph, Earl of Cavan, KP, GCB, GCMG, GCVO, CBE
1931	Brig-Gen Sir George Charles Bingham, 5th Earl of Lucan, KBE, CB, TD (Rifle Brigade) (2)
	EDWARD VIII, 1936
	Brig-Gen Sir George Charles Bingham, 5th Earl of Lucan, KBE, CB, TD (Rifle Brigade)
	GEORGE VI, 1936-1952
	Brig-Gen Sir George Charles Bingham, 5th Earl of Lucan, KBE, CB, TD (Rifle Brigade)
1940	Henry, Baron Snell, CH,CBE (Died 21 Apr 1944)
1945 Nov 5	Colonel Hugh William, 5th Earl Fortescue, OBE,MC (Royal Scots Greys) (1) (Note his increase in Post Nominals below)
1945 Aug 4	Charles George, Baron Ammon, (resigned 21 Jul 1949)
1949	George Robert, Baron Shepherd. (Captain Yeomen of the Guard Jul-Oct 1949)
1951	Colonel Hugh William, 5th Earl Fortescue, KG, CB, OBE, MC (Royal Scots Greys) (2)
	ELIZABETH II, 1952
	Colonel Hugh William, 5th Earl Fortescue, KG, CB, PC, OBE, MC (Royal Scots Greys) (Died 16 Jun 1968)
1958	Major Michael John Hicks-Beach, 2nd Earl St. Aldwyn, TD, (The Royal Gloucestershire Hussars) (1)
1964	Malcolm Newton, 2nd Baron Shepherd
1967	Frank Bacon, Baron Beswick
1971	Major Sir Michael John Hicks-Beach, 2nd Earl St. Aldwyn, KBE, TD, (The Royal Gloucestershire Hussars) (2) (Died 29 Jan 1992)
1974	Patricia, Baroness Llewllyn-Davies of Hastoe (Died 6 Nov 1997).
1979	Sir Bertram, Baron Denham, PC (Oxford & Buckinghamshire Light Infantry) (KBE 1991).(Longest unbroken tenure as Captain since the change of name from Gentlemen Pensioners in 1834)
1991	Sir Thomas Alexander, Baron Hesketh, KBE, PC
1993	Nicholas James Christopher Lowther, 2nd Viscount Ullswater, LVO, PC
1994	Thomas Galloway Dunlop de Bliquy, 2nd Baron Strathclyde PC
1997	Denis Victor, Baron Carter of Devizes PC
2002	Bruce Joseph Grocott, Baron Grocott of Telford, PC
2008	Janet Royall, Baroness Royall of Blaisdon PC
2008	Steven Bassam, Baron Bassam of Brighton.

Lieutenants

Date	Name
	HENRY VIII 1509-1547
1509	Sir John Peachy
1522	Sir Ralph Fane
1539	Sir Richard Page
	EDWARD VI 1547-1553
1550	John, Lord Bray
	MARY 1553-1558
	John, Lord Bray
1557	Edward ffytzgarrett
	ELIZABETH I, 1558-1603
	Edward ffytzgarrett
1591	Sir Henry Greye
1603	Sir Allan Percy
	JAMES I 1605-1625
1603	Sir Allan Percy
1606	Henry Howard
1609	Theophilus Edward, Lord Howard of Walden (Promoted Captain)
1614	Sir George Goringe
	CHARLES I, 1625-1649
1630	George, Lord Goring.
	THE COMMONWEALTH, 1649-1660
	CHARLES II, 1660-1685
1669	Sir John Bennett
1681	Francis Villers, Esq.
	JAMES II, 1685-1689
	Francis Villers, Esq.
	WILLIAM & MARY, 1689-1702
1692	Henry Hevingham, Esq.
	ANNE, 1702-1714
	Henry Hevingham, Esq.
1704	William Seymour, Esq.
	GEORGE I, 1714-1727
	William Seymour, Esq.
	GEORGE II, 1727-1760
	William Seymour, Esq.
1733	Henry, Lord Beauclair
1737	Sir Samuel Garrard, Bt.
1745	Sir William Wynne
1756	The Hon. Harbottle Lutkins

Date	Name
	GEORGE III, 1760-1820
1760	Harcourt Powell, Esq. MP.
1763	Sir Robert Goodere
1781	Villers William Lewis, Esq.
1786	Joseph Esdaile, Esq.
1800	Roger Elliott Roberts, Esq.
1806	Philip Lake Godsall, Esq.
1814	William Henderson, Esq.
	GEORGE IV, 1820-1830
	William Henderson, Esq.
	WILLIAM IV, 1830-1837
1830	Henry B. Hendrich, Esq.
1833 May	Thomas Henry, 4th Baron Foley (1) (Also Captain May 1833-Dec 1834)
1834	Samuel Spry, Esq. MP
	VICTORIA, 1837-1901
	Samuel Spry, Esq. MP
1840	The Hon. Sir Edward Butler
1845	Sir Henry Robinson
1848	Sir Matthew Wyatt
1850	Sir James Tyler
1853	Sir William Topham
1878	Lt Colonel Sir Gustavus Hume
1891	Colonel Sir Henry Hugh Oldham
	EDWARD VII, 1901-1910
	Colonel Sir Henry Oldham
	GEORGE V, 1910-1936
	Colonel Sir Henry Oldham
1922	Lt Colonel Sir Henry Fletcher, CVO
1926	Colonel Sir St.John Gore, CB,CVO,CBE
	EDWARD VIII, 1936
	Colonel Sir St.John Gore, CB,CVO,CBE
	GEORGE VI, 1936-1952
	Colonel Sir St.John Gore, CB, CVO, CBE (Resigned)
1938	Brig General Archibald Fraser Home, KCVO, CB, CMG, DSO. (Resigned)
1945	Brig General Robert Hervey Kearsley, CMG, CVO, CBE.
	ELIZABETH II, 1952
1945	Brig General Robert Hervey Kearsley, CMG, CVO, CBE, DSO. (KCVO 1952) (Appointed Extra Equerry 1955)
1955	Lt Colonel The Hon Osbert Vesey, CMG, CVO, CBE. (KCVO 1956)

Date	Name
1956	Major Sir Henry Aubrey-Fletcher, Bt, DSO, MVO. (CVO 1957)
1957	Lt Colonel the Marquess of Ormonde, MC.(CVO 1960)
1963	Major General William Fox-Pitt, DSO, MVO, MC. (CVO 1966)
1966	Brigadier Sir Henry Floyd, Bt, CB,CBE. (Died 1968)
1968	Colonel Sir Robert Gooch, Bt, DSO. (KCVO 1973)
1973	Colonel Kenneth Savill, DSO. (CVO 1976)
1976	Colonel Henry Clowes, DSO, OBE. (CVO 1977, KCVO 1981.)
1981	Colonel Richard John Vesey Chrichton, MC. (CVO 1986)
1986	Major David Jamieson, VC. (CVO 1990)
1990	Major Thomas St.Aubyn. (CVO 1993)
1993	Lt Colonel Sir James Scott, Bt. (Died 1993)
1993	Brigadier Alan Breitmeyer
1994	Colonel Thomas Hall, OBE (CVO 1997)
1998	Lt Colonel Richard Mayfield, DSO (LVO 2000)
2000	Colonel David Fanshawe, OBE. (LVO 2003)
2003	Major Barnaby Cockcroft (LVO 2006)
2006	Lt Colonel the Hon Guy Norrie

Standard Bearer

Date	Name
	HENRY VIII 1509-1547
1509	
1526	Edward Billingham
1539	Sir Thomas Darcy
	EDWARD VI 1547-1553
1547	John Cavarley
1550	Sir William Stafford
	MARY 1553-1558
	Sir William Stafford
1557	Sir William Suliard
	ELIZABETH I, 1558-1603
	Sir William Suliard
1561	Thomas Marsham
1577	Sir Charles Somerset
1600	Sir John Scudamore
1604	Sir William Harvie
	JAMES I 1605-1625
	Sir William Harvie
1618	Sir Edward Capell
	CHARLES I, 1625-1649
	Not known
	THE COMMONWEALTH, 1649-1660
	Not known
	CHARLES II, 1660-1685
	Not known
1669	Sir John Walpool
1677	Francis Villers, Esq.
1681	Sir Humphrey Sturt
	JAMES II, 1685-1689
1685	Sir Thomas Bludworth
	WILLIAM & MARY, 1689-1702
	Sir Thomas Bludworth
1692	Boucher Fane, Esq.
1700	Charles Fane, Esq.
	ANNE, 1702-1714
	Charles Fane, Esq.
1712	The Hon. John West

Date	Name
	GEORGE I, 1714-1727
	The Hon. John West
1716	William Wynne, Esq. (Promoted Lieut 1745)
	GEORGE II, 1727-1760
	William Wynne, Esq. (Promoted Lieut 1745)
1745-48	Not known
1748	The Hon. Harbottle Grimston
1751	Harcourt Powell, Esq.
	GEORGE III, 1760-1820
1760	John Bridger, (Jun)
1768	John Lee Warner, Esq.
1789	William Greene, Esq.
1790	Edward Boscowen Frederick, Esq
1806	Edward Dawson, Esq.
1818	John Stockdale, Esq.
	GEORGE IV, 1820-1830
1820	George Pocock, Esq.
	WILLIAM IV, 1830-1837
	George Pocock, Esq.
	VICTORIA, 1837-1901
	George Pocock, Esq.
1840	Henry Robinson, Esq.
1850	Major David James Harmer (First military officer in the Hon Corps). Appointed directly as Standard Bearer
1872	Lt Colonel William McCall
1876	Major William O'Bryen Taylor
1886	Major Philip Limborch Tillbrook
1900	Colonel Aubone G.Fife
	EDWARD VII, 1901-1910
	Colonel Aubone G.Fife
	GEORGE V, 1910-1936
	Colonel Aubone G. Fife
1920	Lt Colonel Sir Henry Fletcher, CVO (Promoted Lieut)
1922	Colonel St.John Corbett Gore, CB, CBE
1926	Colonel Wilford Neville Lloyd, CB, CVO (Promoted Lieut 1926)
1935	Brig General Archibald Fraser Home, CB,CMG, CVO, DSO (Promoted Lieut 1938)

Date	Name
	EDWARD VIII, 1936
	Brig General Archibald Fraser Home, CB, CMG, CVO, DSO (Promoted Lieut 1938)
	GEORGE VI, 1936-1952
1938	Brig General Sir Frederick Gascoigne, KCVO, CMG, DSO (Died 1944)
1945	Colonel Ulric Thynne, CMG, DSO,TD. (Retired CVO 1945)
1946	Brig General Basil Buckley, CB, CMG. (Retired (CVO 1949)
1949	Colonel Henry Pryce-Jones, CB, DSO, MVO, MC (Resigned CVO 1952)
	ELIZABETH II, 1952
1952	Major General The Hon Maurice Wingfield, CMG, DSO. (CVO 1953)
1953	Lt Colonel The Hon Osbert Vesey, CMG, CVO, CBE (Promoted Lieut)
1955	Major Sir Henry Aubrey-Fletcher, Bt, DSO, MVO. (Promoted Lieut)
1956	Colonel Sir Bartle Edwards, MC. (Retired, CVO 1961, Knight Bachelor 1956)
1961	Major General William Fox-Pitt, DSO, MVO, MC. (Promoted Lieut)
1963	Brigadier Sir Henry Floyd, Bt, CB, CBE. (Promoted Lieut)
1966	Brigadier John Cheney, OBE. (Retired, CVO 1967)
1967	Colonel Sir Robert Gooch, Bt, DSO. (Promoted Lieut)
1968	Colonel Sir John Carew Pole, Bt, DSO, TD
1972	Colonel Kenneth Savill, DSO (Promoted Lieut)
1973	Colonel Henry Clowes, DSO, OBE. (Promoted Lieut)
1976	Colonel Samuel Enderby, DSO, MC. (Retired CVO 1977)
1977	Brigadier The Hon Richard Hamilton-Russell, DSO. (MVO 1977)
1979	Lt Colonel Peter Clifton, DSO. (CVO 1980)
1981	Major Derek Allhusen (CVO 1984)
1984	Major The Marquess of Donegall (LVO 1986)
1986	Colonel James Eagles (LVO 1988)
1988	Colonel Anthony Way, MC.
1990	Lt Colonel Sir James Scott, Bt. (Promoted Lieut)
1993	Major Sir Fergus Matheson of Matheson, Bt.
1997	Colonel Sir Piers Bengough, KCVO, OBE
1999	Major Anthony Arkwright
2000	Major Sir Timothy Gooch, Bt. (Resigned)
2003	Colonel James Baker, MBE
2008	Colonel Sir William Mahon, Bt

Clerk of the Cheque

Date	Name
	HENRY VIII 1509-1547
1509	
1526	William Birch
	EDWARD VI 1547-1553
	William Birch
1548	John Pyers
	MARY 1553-1558
	John Pyers
1554	John Moore
	ELIZABETH I, 1558-1603
	John Moore. Retirement date unknown
1577	Robert Hall
1585	Bonaventie Ashbie
	JAMES I 1605-1625
1604	Thomas Stapley, Esq.
1609	Richard Greene, Esq.
	CHARLES I, 1625-1649
	Not known
	THE COMMONWEALTH, 1649-1660
	Not known
	CHARLES II, 1660-1685
	Not known
1669	Thomas Wynne, Esq.
1681	William Thomas, Esq.
	JAMES II, 1685-1689
	Not known
	WILLIAM & MARY, 1689-1702
1690	Robert Manley, Esq.
	ANNE, 1702-1714
1711	Philip Pendock, Esq.
	GEORGE I, 1714-1727
1724	George Turner, Esq.
	GEORGE II, 1727-1760
1753	Joseph Nicholas Smith, Esq.
	GEORGE III, 1760-1820
1760	Charles Cecil Calvert, Esq
1768	William Desse, Esq.
1773	Thomas Hayward, Esq.

Date	Name
1779	William Lybbe Powys, Esq.
1813	Henry Philip Powys, Esq.
1815	Jospeh Wells, Esq.
	GEORGE IV, 1820-1830
1820	Joseph Glossop, Esq.
1824	Thomas Hancock, Esq.
	WILLIAM IV, 1830-1837
1834	Albert William Beetham, Esq.
	VICTORIA, 1837-1901
1838	James Bunce Curling, Esq.
1852	Joseph Skipp Lloyd, Esq.
1856	William Walter Cargill, Esq.
1863	Lt Colonel William McCall (Promoted Standard Bearer 1872) First military Clerk of the Cheque and Adjutant
1872	Major William O'Bryen Taylor (Promoted Standard Bearer 1876)
1876	Lt Colonel Gustavus Hume (Promoted Lieut 1878)
1878	Major Philip Limborch Tillbrook (Promoted Standard Bearer 1886)
1887	Lt Colonel John Hobart Culme-Seymour
1887	Colonel Henry Hugh Oldham (Promoted Lieut 1891) (Joined in 1887)
1891	Colonel Aubone G.Fife (Promoted Standard Bearer 1900)
1900	Colonel Henry A. Fletcher. (Promoted Standard Bearer 1920, and Lieut 1922)
	EDWARD VII, 1901-1910
	Colonel Henry A.Fletcher. (Promoted Standard Bearer 1920, and Lieut 1922)
	GEORGE V, 1910-1936
	Colonel Henry A Fletcher. (Promoted Standard Bearer 1920, and Lieut 1922)
1920	Colonel St.John Corbett Gore, CB, CBE (Promoted Standard Bearer 1922)
1922	Lt Colonel Charles Ferguson Campbell, CIE, OBE.
1925	Colonel Wilford Neville Lloyd, CB, CVO (Promoted Lieut 1926)
1926	Brig General Archibald Fraser Home, CB, CMG, CVO, DSO (Promoted Lieut 1938)
1935	Brig General Robert Hervey Kearsley, CMG, DSO
	EDWARD VIII, 1936
	Brig General Robert Hervey Kearsley, CMG,DSO
	GEORGE VI, 1936-1952
	Brig General Robert Hervey Kearsley, CMG, DSO

Date	Name
1945	Lt Colonel Valentine Vivian, CMG, DSO, MVO (Died 1948)
1948	Lt Colonel The Hon Osbert Vesey, CBE (Promoted Standard Bearer 1953, Lieut 1955)
	ELIZABETH II, 1952
	Lt Colonel The Hon Osbert Vesey, CBE (Promoted Standard Bearer 1953, Lieut 1955)
1953	Lt Colonel the Marquess of Ormonde, MC.(Promoted Lieut 1957)
1957	Brigadier Sir Henry Floyd, Bt, CB, CBE. (Promoted Standard Bearer 1963, Lieut 1966)
1963	Colonel Sir Robert Gooch, Bt, DSO. (Promoted Standard Bearer 1967, Lieut 1968)
1967	Colonel Henry Clowes, MC. (Promoted Standard Bearer 1973. Lieut 1976)
1973	Lt Colonel Peter Clifton, DSO. (Promoted Standard Bearer 1979)
1979	Lt Colonel Richard Chrichton, MC. (Promoted Lieut 1981)
1980	Major David Jamieson VC. (Promoted Lieut 1986)
1986	Major Thomas St.Aubyn. (Promoted Lieut 1990)
1990	Major Sir Torquhil Matheson of Matheson, Bt. (Died 1993).
1993	Colonel Thomas Hall, OBE (Promoted Lieut 1994).
1994	Lt Colonel Richard Mayfield, DSO. (Promoted Lieut 1998)
1998	Colonel David Fanshawe, OBE. (Promoted Lieut 1999)
1999	Major Barnaby Cockcroft (Promoted Lieut 2003)
2003	Lt Colonel the Hon Guy Norrie (Promoted Lieut 2006)
2006	Colonel Sir William Mahon, Bt (Promoted Standard Bearer 2008)
2008	Lt Colonel Peter Chamberlin

Harbinger

Date	Name
	HENRY VIII 1509-1547
1509	
1526	John More
1539	John Stephans
	EDWARD VI 1547-1553
	John Stephans?
	MARY 1553-1558
	John Stephans?
1557	John Somterley
	ELIZABETH I, 1558-1603
	John Moore. Retirement date unknown
1561	Bonaventie Ashbie (Clerk of the Cheque 1585)
	(Successor not identified)
1591	Thomas Bellingham
1599	Thomas Stapley.
1604	William Ashbie
	JAMES I 1605-1625
1604	William Ashbie
	CHARLES I, 1625-1649
	Not known
	THE COMMONWEALTH, 1649-1660
	Not known
	CHARLES II, 1660-1685
	Not known
1669	Richard Child, Esq.
	JAMES II, 1685-1689
	Not known
	WILLIAM & MARY, 1689-1702
1692	George Shipway
1700	Richard Rusby
	ANNE, 1702-1714
1704	Richard Reeves, Esq.
	GEORGE I, 1714-1727
1723	Matthew Gossett (Retirement date unknown)
	GEORGE II, 1727-1760
1737	John Bap
1751	George Chauvel
	GEORGE III, 1760-1820
1768	Charles Friday

Date	Name
1787	John Webb
1789	S.Boulding.
1807	J.A.Oliver
1819	William M.Thistleton, Esq.
	GEORGE IV, 1820-1830
1822	Robert F.Grosso, Esq.
1830	Samuel Wilson, Esq
	WILLIAM IV, 1830-1837
	Samuel Wilson, Esq
	VICTORIA, 1837-1901
1848	Sub Officer Instituted. During the period of overlap with the Harbinger the Sub Officer is shown in italics.
1848	Major P.Percy Neville (Retired 1859; Sub-Officer vacancy not immediately filled)
After 1859	Lt Colonel John Henry Cooke (Sub-Officer)
1863	Capt George Nathaniel Philips (Sub-Officer)
	Samuel Wilson, Esq., retired as Harbinger. OFFICE OF HARBINGER ABOLISHED 5th July 1865
1874	Lt Colonel John Glas Sandeman (Sub-Officer)
	EDWARD VII, 1901-1910
	Lt Colonel John Glas Sandeman (Sub-Officer)
	GEORGE V, 1910-1936
	Lt Colonel John Glas Sandeman (Sub-Officer)
1912	Lt Colonel William Angel Scott
	NAME OF OFFICE CHANGED TO GENTLEMAN HARBINGER Dec 7th 1927. (i.e. Not an Officer of the Hon Corps)
1927	Lt Colonel William Angel Scott
1932	Brig General Sir Frederick Gascoigne, KCVO, CMG, DSO (Promoted Standard Bearer 1938)
	EDWARD VIII, 1936
	Brig General Sir Frederick Gascoigne, KCVO, CMG, DSO (Promoted Standard Bearer 1938)
	GEORGE VI, 1936-1952
	Brig General Sir Frederick Gascoigne, KCVO, CMG, DSO (Promoted Standard Bearer 1938)
1938	Colonel Henry Pryce-Jones, DSO, MVO, MC (CB 1943, Resigned CVO 1952)
1949	Maj General The Hon Maurice Wingfield, CMG, DSO. (Promoted Standard Bearer 1952)

Hon Mess Secretary

Date	Name
	ELIZABETH II, 1952
1952	Maj General Arthur Chater, CB,DSO,OBE
	HARBINGER APPOINTMENT RAISED TO OFFICER STATUS, 1965
1965	Maj General Arthur Chater, CB, DSO, OBE (CVO 1966)
1966	Lt Colonel John Chandos-Pole, OBE. (CVO 1979)
1979	Colonel Ivo Reid, OBE
1981	Lt Colonel James Eagles (Promoted Standard Bearer 1986, LVO 1988)
1986	Colonel Philip Pardoe (Died 1987)
1987	Lt Colonel Robert Steele, MBE
1990	Major The Lord Suffield, MC
1992	Brigadier Alan Breitmeyer (Promoted Lieutenant 1993)
1993	Major Sir Philip Duncombe, Bt.
1997	Major Mervyn Colenso-Jones
2000	Colonel James Baker, MBE (Promoted Standard Bearer 2003)
2003	Major Carol Gurney
2006	Colonel Robert ffrench Blake

Note: Early Harbingers are distingushed in this list as Gentlemen (with no post-nominal description), or the superior social rank of Esquire.

Date	Name
1878-1897	Colonel J.A. Stewart
1898-1900	Lt Colonel H.Fletcher
1901-1905	Major Hon W. Rowley
1906-1919	Lt Colonel Angel Scott
1920-1922	Colonel C Campbell
1923	Colonel C de W Crookshank
1924-1932	Brig General Marsdin Newton
1924-1932	Brig General H. Kearsley
1935	Col H. Pryce-Jones
1938	Lt Colonel C. Gray (Died 1945)
1946	Lt Colonel Victor Daly
1947	Brig General Basil Buckley
1949	Lt Colonel Kenneth Previté
1951	Maj General Arthur Chater
1959	Lt Colonel John Chandos-Pole
1966	Colonel Henry Clowes
1967	Lt Colonel George Kidston-Montgomerie of Southannon
1968	Colonel Peter Clifton
1974	Colonel Ivo Reid
1977	Colonel Richard Crichton
1979	Major David Jamieson VC
1982	Colonel Philip Pardoe
1984	Major Thomas St.Aubyn
1986	Major Sir Torquhil Matheson of Matheson, Bt.
1989	Colonel Thomas Hall
1992	Lt Colonel Richard Mayfield
1994	Major Mervyn Colenso-Jones
1996	Colonel David Fanshawe
1998	Major Sir Timothy Gooch, Bt.
2000	Major Carol Gurney
2001	Lt Colonel the Hon Guy Norrie
2003	Colonel Sir William Mahon, Bt.
2006	Lt Colonel Peter Chamberlin
2008	Maj General Jonathan Hall

Axe Keeper

Date	Name
	ANNE, 1702-1714
1712	Mr Charles Hayes
	GEORGE I, 1714-1727
	Mr Charles Hayes
	GEORGE II, 1727-1760
	Mr Charles Hayes
1729	Mr William Baldwin
1748	Mr Thomas Duncomb
1751	Mr Thomas Hodgson
1756	Mr Thomas Higgs
	GEORGE III, 1760-1820
1760	Mr John Clarke
1762	Mr James Walker
1791	Mr Richard Scafe
1806	Mr Robert Thorp
1819	Mr Richard Hill
	GEORGE IV, 1820-1830
	Mr Richard Hill
1829	Mr R.Howe
	WILLIAM IV, 1830-1837
	Mr R.Howe
1834	Mr Thomas Whiteman
	VICTORIA, 1837-1901
	Mr Thomas Whiteman
1849	Mr Thomas Masters
1866	Mr Samuel Jaens
1868	Mr John Towers
	EDWARD VII, 1901-1910
	Mr John Towers
1908	Mr G.Mason Petit
	GEORGE V, 1910-1936
1933	Mr Henry Harrison
	EDWARD VIII, 1936
	Mr Henry Harrison
	GEORGE VI, 1936-1952
	Mr Henry Harrison
1951	Mr Ernest Marsh
	ELIZABETH II, 1952
	Mr Ernest Marsh (Resigned for health reasons)

Date	Name
1956	Mr Mark Charles Smith, Irish Guards (Deceased)
1973	Mr John Armstrong, Coldstream Guards. (RVM, 1985)
1985	Mr James Richards, Welsh Guards
1989	Mr Alan Edwin Hayter, Scots Guards
2001	Major Patrick Verdon, Royal Artillery

Notes & Bibliography

To avoid needless repetition, a source used more than once is abbreviated in **bold** type for subsequent reference, both below and in the various Boxes.

1 'Who's Who in History', ed **Routh**, Vol II p 31.

2 A.F.Pollard's '**Henry VIII**'.

3 The Corps went under a confusing variety of names during the early centuries of its long history. For the sake of simplicity, if at the cost of strict historical accuracy, the term 'Body Guard' is hereafter used, unless there seems some special point in doing otherwise. (I choose to make it two words, rather than one, as some authorities do, and am aware that I have it sometimes singular, sometimes plural, as context and comfort seem to favour!)

4 This quotation and the one in the following paragraph come from pages 32 and 34 of 'The Nearest Guard', by Major Henry **Brackenbury**. This invaluable source was written by a Gentleman-at-Arms just before the 400th anniversary.

5 'The Spears of Honour and The Gentlemen Pensioners', a pamphlet published privately in 1912 by Colonel John Glas Sandeman, a Gentleman-at-arms, purports to prove that the original Body Guard was disbanded in 1515, and re-formed in 1539, and that it took no part in the Battle of the Spurs or the Field of the Cloth of Gold. This is not a proposition that survives scrutiny, and has not been taken up, indeed has not been mentioned, by any other authority. Since it exists in print we mention it here.

6 'History of England', GM **Trevelyan**, p 313.

7 'The Story of Britain' by Sir Roy **Strong** p 185, © 1996 Oman Productions Ltd.

8 **Brackenbury**, p 47.

9 'The Archaeological Journal' (**AJ**) Vol XCIII, C deW **Crookshank**.

10 'His Majesty's Bodyguard', Harvey **Kearsley**, p 8. Published in 1937, this is another invaluable source document. Clerk of the Cheque and Adjutant, Brig Gen Harvey Kearsley listed and put in order all the Body Guard's surviving records.

11 'The Sisters who Would be Queen' by Leanda **de Lisle** p128.

12 **Churchill**, ' History of the English Speaking Peoples', Vol II, p 81.

13 **Brackenbury** p 62.

14 **AJ**, p 4.

15 **Strong**, pp 191 & 205.

16 **Routh**, p 225.

17 **Brackenbury** pp 102/5.

18 Henry IV's dismissive description of his brother monarch, possibly borrowed from the Duc de Sully.

19 **Brackenbury** p 109.

20 **Brackenbury** p 154.

21 **Strong** p 297.

22 **Brackenbury** p 177.

23 **Churchill** Vol III p 106.

24 **Kearsley** p 34.

25 'George III' by Christopher Hibbert (Penguin) ch 27.

26 'Robert Peel' by Douglas Hurd p 91

27 **Brackenbury** p 178.

28 **Churchill** Vol IV p 32.

29 Oxford **D**ictionary of **N**ational **B**iography.

30 **Kearsley** p 46.

31 'Victoria's Wars' by Saul David – an absolutely excellent source, generously illustrated, which I have drawn on freely.

32 **de Lisle** p 123.

33 For details of Body Guard VCs, as well as for much help and friendly encouragement, I am much indebted to the Standard Bearer, Colonel Sir William Mahon Bt.

34 **Churchill**, Vol IV, p 296.

35 An engaging rationale of this debacle is to be found in 'On The Psychology of Military Incompetence' by Norman Dixon, ch 4.

36 **Kearsley**, p 191.

37 Contemporary newspaper accounts tell of how word of the delay broke when the Bishop of London was actually rehearsing the ceremony in Westminster Abbey, presumably with the Body Guard taking part. "With great presence of mind he promptly held a service of intercession for the King's complete restoration to health" – Longman's 'Chronicle of the 20th Century'.

38 **Brackenbury**, p 199.

39 **Kearsley** p 61.

39 'The Good Soldier' by Gary Mead, p 173.

40 Order Book VI, pp 221 *et seq*.

41 Major Sir Fergus Matheson of Matheson's 'Digest'.

42 'Walking the London Blitz' by Clive Harris, p 77.

43 'Soldier' magazine, 1949.

Illustrations and photographs are reproduced by kind permission of the following:

The Royal Collection © 2008, Her Majesty Queen Elizabeth II –

Page 5 'King Henry VIII' after Hans Holbein the Younger. RCIN 404107

Pags 6-7 'The Battle of the Spurs'. Flemish School, painted about 1513 for Henry VIII. RCIN 406784

Page 9 'King Edward VI (1537-53)'. Possibly painted by William Scrots who was employed by Henry VIII from 1545. RCIN 403452

Page 13 'Elizabeth I' (1533-1603). British School, painted 1580-1585. First recorded in the Royal Collection in the reign of William IV. RCIN 405749

Pages 18-19 'A View of Greenwich' 1632 by Adriaen van Stalbemt (1580-1662) with Jan van Belcamp (died c.1652) for King Charles I. RCIN 405291

Pages 20-21 'Hampton Court Palace' about 1640. British School. Acquired by King George V. RCIN 405791

Pages 24-25 'Embarkation of Henry VIII'. British School, painted between 1520 and 1540, for Henry VIII. RCIN 405793

Pages26-27 'The Field of Cloth of Gold, 1520'. British School, presumably painted for Henry VIII. RCIN 405794

Page 27 'Francis I, King of France, 1494-1547'. First recorded in the Royal Collection in the time of Charles I. RCIN 403433

Page 36 'King James VI and I, (1566-1625)' by Paul van Somer in 1618. Sold in 1651, but recovered for Charles II in 1660. RCIN 401224

Page 37 'King Charles I from Three Angles' by Sir Anthony van Dyck, painted in 1635. RCIN 404420

Page 38 'King Charles II' (1630-1685) by John Michael Wright probably in 1661.RCIN 404951

Page 42 'King William III' (1650-1702) by Sir Godfrey Kneller. Possibly part of a fragment from the wall paintings at Windsor, preserved by Sir Jeffrey Wyatville during restoration work at the Castle. RCIN 404327

Page 44 'Queen Anne' (1665-1714). Painted by Sir Godfrey Kneller in 1702-4. Purchased by HM The Queen. RCIN 405614

Page 44 'King George I' (1660-1727) by Kneller in 1715. RCIN 405677

Page 46 'King George II' (1683-1760). British School. (First recorded in the Royal Collection in the reign of Queen Victoria). RCIN 406588

Page 48 'King George III' (1783-1820) by Zoffany, painted in 1771. RCIN 405072.

Page 49 'King George III's Procession to Parliament' by John Wootton, painted in 1762. Purchased for the Royal Collection by King George IV. RCIN 402002

Page 52 'King George IV as Prince of Wales' by Miltenberg after Gainsborough. RCIN 421947

Page 54 'King William IV' by Johan Georg Paul Fischer. RCIN 420217

Page 55 'The Honourable Band of Gentlemen Pensioners' by Alexandre-Jean Dubois Drahonet. Commissioned by King William IV. RCIN 407002

Page 66 'Queen Victoria' (1819-1901) by Mrs Koberwein-Terrel, probably painted for Queen Mary. RCIN 404462

Page 72 'The Queen, riding Sunset, distributing the first Victoria Crosses' by George Housman Thomas (1824-68). RL 16806

Page 74 'God Save The Queen': (Queen Victoria arriving at St Paul's Cathedral on the occasion of the Diamond) by John Charlton. RCIN 400211

Page 76 'The Queen's Garden Party, 28 June 1897', by Laurits Regner Tuxen. Commissioned by Queen Victoria. RCIN 405286

Page 96 'King Edward VII' (1841-1910) by John Lewis Reilly. Commissioned by King Edward VII. RCIN 401061

Page 100 'A Levee at St James's Palace' by Messrs Dickinson, 1902-1905.RCIN 407149

Page 104 'King George V' (1865-1936) by Richard Jack. RCIN 404547

Page 106 'The Unveiling of the Queen Victoria Memorial' 16 May 1911 by Sydney Pryor Hall. RCIN 404351

Page 110 'King George VI' (1895-1952) (as Admiral of the Fleet) by Denis Quintin Fildes. RCIN 409162

Page 112 'Queen Elizabeth The Queen Mother' (1900-2002) by Sir Gerald Festus Kelly. RCIN 403423

Page 120 'The Coronation of Queen Elizabeth II' by Terence Cuneo (1907-96).RCIN 404470

The Bridgeman Art Library © – *Page 8* 'The Execution of Lady Jane Grey' (oil on canvas 1833) by Delaroche, Hippolyte (Paul) (1797-1856) National Gallery, London. *Page 10* 'Queen Mary (1516-58) and Princess Elizabeth (1533-1603) entering London, 1553' 1910 (fresco) by Shaw, John Byam Liston (1872-1919) Houses of Parliament, , London

Crown Copyright – *pages viii*, 29, 131-137 © Crown Copyright/MOD. Reproduced with the permission of the Controller of Her Majesty's Stationery Office.

Ministry of Defence Art Collection © – *Page 81* 'Survivors of the Crimea and Indian Mutiny' by Sir Arthur Felix Temple Clay

From the collection of the Walker Art Gallery, courtesy **National Museums Liverpool**© – *Pages 60-61* ''The Eve of the Battle of Edgehill, 1642' 1845 Charles Landseer (1799 - 1879)

Press Association © – *Cover* Quincentennial Parade 2009

Steve Solomons © – *Page 139* Group photograph 2009

Mr J K Wingfield Digby of Sherborne Castle © *Page 16* 'The Procession of Queen Elizabeth 1'

Victoria & Albert Museum London © V&A Images – *Page 70* 'The Opening of the Great Exhibition'

The remainder of the images are from the Body Guard's own collection and archives and have been photographed by Misha Anikst.